Money Secrets with Bill & Mike

by

Michael Tove & Bill Alexander

Written by Michael Tove & Bill Alexander
ISBN-10: 1-970114-04-5
ISBN-13: 978-1-970114-04-1

Production Services by Erica Smith

TABLE OF CONTENTS

PREFACE

In the world of professional advisors, both Legal and Financial, some are better than most and a few outperform all others. We believe that every professional should strive for excellence. Certainly, there are highly skilled professionals who deliver excellent counsel and advice to their clients with integrity, due diligence and care. People who receive and follow advice from these exceptional professionals will materially benefit from that relationship. Unfortunately, not every advisor shares our devotion to excellence. Sometimes they lack specific training, including advanced training. Sometimes they just don't listen to you. Sometimes they have an artificial bias for or against a particular strategy or set of solutions, perhaps because of limitations imposed by their employers, including competitive pressures to always recommend one thing over another. Sometimes they're more concerned with how much money they can make rather than what is in your best interest consistent with your risk tolerance. But whether by accident or design these biased recommendations fail to serve clients in the very best way possible.

One bad experience can push people without adequate experience or knowledge to "go it alone." That creates another problem. Far too often people mistakenly believe that they can acquire all the facts necessary from well-meaning friends and relatives, or articles they find online or read in magazines or listening to media jocks. The details and fine-print matter and sometimes what's not stated is more important than what is. Often, two seemingly identical plans can have vastly different results related to the most inconspicuous of differences.

Because we know how complex it seems to understand the markets or make good investment decisions regarding your money, or even to choose an advisor, we started a TV Program entitled *Money Secrets with Bill & Mike*. This half-hour weekly show explores a wide array of topics related to matters of financial planning, asset protection, wealth transfer, tax considerations, and so forth. Sometimes we disagree but by and large, coming from different directions, we find that our many years of experience results in similar advice to our clients—Bill as an Advisor and Attorney and Mike as a Financial Advisor, both focused on asset protection and preservation, and above all, planning before products. We are especially united when it comes to our mission to materially improve the lives of every client who works with either of us. We firmly believe that everyone deserves excellence in planning and that just because someone is "doing okay" does not mean they can't do better.

Therefore, as a companion to our show *Money Secrets with Bill & Mike*, we've decided to collaborate on a book of the same title. This volume will summarize each show as a chapter, in sequence to how they aired. Like the episodes of our show, each chapter will explore one topic, discuss the issues, the mistakes that people commonly make and conclude with our "Money Secret." However, where a TV show is limited by air time constraints, a book has no such limitation. Thus, we can use these pages to expand and elaborate on aspects that could not be covered on the show.

Nothing in this book is intended to serve as specific legal, tax or financial advice and no one should substitute this book for professional counsel or advice on any matter. Rather, the purpose of this book, like the television show, is to provide general educational guidance to the public at large and encourage everyone to become better informed. Then, armed with that extra knowledge, you can seek good professional advice and take the action that's best for you.

This final point is the ultimate "Money Secret" for every topic we cover. Professional, individual advice simply cannot be properly dispensed in advance of a thorough process of discovery and due diligence between a client and an advisor.

CHAPTER 1
DON'T BE A DO IT YOURSELFER

We've heard it all before:

- "*Don't hire an expensive attorney. The online software for a fraction of the cost is just as good.*"
- "*Don't pay those high asset management fees when you can get all the investments you need for a flat charge per trade.*"
- "*I know as much about investing as any professional fund manager.*"
- "*I don't need insurance. I can handle whatever happens by myself.*" or "*My family will come to my rescue.*" etc.
- "*Those advisors* (attorneys, CPAs, insurance agents, investment advisors, etc.) *are all out to get you.*"
- "_____ (your favorite internet author or media personality) *says I should* (do this and such)."

Far too often, people mistakenly believe that they can acquire all the information necessary to complete their planning from non-professional sources including well-meaning friends and relatives, articles they find online, things they read in magazines, or hear from media jocks. And far too often, the consequences of these decisions are disastrous. For better or worse, good planning is complex, not because it's hard to understand or that any given plan is terribly convoluted, but because the number of possible plans—whether legal, financial, etc. are as numerous as the number of people alive. In other words, the range of possibilities is infinite.

Let's start with a simple premise:

If you fail to plan, you plan to fail.

Too many people have no legal documents, no formal financial plan and they're truly at risk. Invariably, this mistake stems from one of three sources:

1. The mistaken belief that planning is for someone else (with more wealth, a better job, bigger house, etc.).
2. They see little value in planning and don't want to spend money on something they don't understand.
3. Procrastination.

The biggest irony with non-planning, is how many of these people decry that the last thing they want is for the "*government to get their grubby hands on my money*" but that is precisely what no planning invites.

Many people feel they can find boiler plate legal documents, financial plans, etc. There are a lot of justifications for this, but by and large, it boils down to not wanting to spend the money they think it'll cost to do the planning. Sadly, good planning often costs a lot less than you think and in the end, actually costs *less* than not having a good plan. This error is not helped by the mass-marketed one-size fits all recommendations that bombard us from all quarters, including print media, radio, television and internet. The fact that many people have the same needs does not mean they should all use the same plan. Just as no two individuals are identical, neither should all plans and recommendations be identical. Plans that differ by even imperceptible degrees can offer dramatically different results, even when called the same thing.

Planning Tools come in many forms. Some are items (products) that we purchase. Some are strategies of how to use those products. They're all tools. Tools are important but only to the extent that they accomplish a needed job. Nobody would doubt that a hammer is an important tool for a carpenter but it's a poor choice if what's needed is cutting the board.

Legal Documents—

Wills vs. Trusts. Wills are governed by state statutes, meaning they are regulated by the states. The laws of inheritance and what makes a valid Will, differ from state to state. As such, a Will drafted in one state may not be fully applicable in another. In addition, property must be probated in the state where it is owned, not in the state where the owner lived, if different. Thus, owning properties in different states means those assets will be probated separately according to each state's laws of probate and administration. The difference between a Will that works and one that doesn't can be as simple as a few sentences of text. When you move from one state to another, don't assume your documents will work. You should always have your Will and other legal documents reviewed in your new state by an estate planning attorney in *that* state.

Conversely, Trusts are documents that can transcend state boundaries with minor amendments. However, there are many different variations of trusts and even the most basic can have dramatic differences from one to the next. Generally, trusts best serve those families in need of more than basic planning—second marriages, children by previous marriages, issues with estate or income tax, the need for asset protection, avoiding multiple probates, complex assets such as business assets, government assistance planning, or simply wanting the privacy, speed, and lower costs associated with estate settlement that comes with trusts.

Within the broad framework of estate planning, some people are well served by good Will-based planning while others are better served by Trust-based planning. The differences can relate to such simple variables as current and former marital status, type of assets owned and where it is located, who the beneficiaries are including their marital status, whether you are looking for asset protection for your family, how much control you wish to exercise over inherited assets, and a myriad of other variables.

Powers of Attorney. These are "life planning" documents, that if properly drafted, allow your family to avoid the time and expense of Guardianship. The fact is that "life planning" can be more complex and far more important than "death planning." Many people are not familiar with these important documents much less recognize that they're essential to good planning.

Powers of Attorney allow you to choose your own agent, authorize your designated persons to make legal, financial and medical decisions on your behalf when you are legally or functionally unable to do so. Unfortunately, most seniors who already have Powers of Attorney don't have the *right* Powers in place for even basic asset protection planning when things go wrong. Having the right Powers of Attorney can not only mean the difference in your assets being used in the way you want, but literally can be the difference between life or death.

Many Powers of Attorney are drafted with only the most rudimentary considerations being addressed. Others are more robust and cover any reasonable contingency. The difference between the good ones and all the rest can be very subtle and the common person may not notice the difference. But, when it comes to their use, the devil is always in the details and when a Power of Attorney is needed, by definition, it's too late to fix what's broken.

The sad truth is that most people do not have the legal knowledge or skill to know the difference between good or bad legal documents. They must "trust" their attorney to give them the documents they need. But unfortunately most attorneys, even many estate planning attorneys lack experience with asset protection planning or government assistance for long term care needs that most families need. The real tragedy is that good documents and poor documents can cost the same to prepare. So how can you tell the difference?

Before retaining a legal planning advisor, particularly if you're nearing retirement or older, check credentials. Seek someone with expertise in Asset Protection (estate planning, tax planning) and Elder Law. Then interview them. As important as credentials are, it's also important to work with someone who focuses on your best interests and with whom you're comfortable.

Financial Planning—

There is no such thing as One and Done. But too often, someone will buy a series of financial products guard them with near religious fervor, and never consider making changes. While there is a lot to be said for the virtue of loyalty, the larger question is this: are you more loyal to that favorite product than that product is loyal to you?

The opposite is equally problematic. Some people chase returns so vigorously they become amateur "day traders." Ironically, many professional fund managers do less day-to-day trading. Also, professionals who do trade frequently have actual brokers on the floor of the stock exchanges, ready to make their trades. The rest of us do not and must rely on "middle men" who are those professionals. This is not the arena of the investment "weekend warrior."

On occasion, active day-traders do well, but by and large, the data show that for every one who does well, many more don't. For example, multiple studies from Dalbar (a Boston-based financial research group) and Morningstar have consistently shown most active traders under-perform "buy and hold" investors, especially when taxes and transaction fees are added into the equation. Most self-traders are also unaware of the breadth and depth of different financial products that exist—or the considerations that smart planning requires.

Market Investments. The vast majority of investment portfolios, especially retirement plans (IRAs, 401k's, etc.) are fundamentally similar, offering roughly the same mixes of stocks, bonds and mutual funds. Unfortunately, over the past 20 years, in light of the ever-tightening realm of digital instant communication, markets with seemingly vastly different objectives (large vs. small company, growth vs. value, domestic vs. international, etc.) have come to move in lockstep with each other. Thus, the ability for an investment portfolio to truly be diversified has diminished. Owning two investments that perform identically is no better than owning one, but can increase managing costs with no net benefit. Fundamentally, you cannot eliminate stock market risk by being invested in the stock markets regardless of how many investment components you have.

Annuities. Many insurance-licensed agents tout annuities as alternatives to market investments, including as the *only* alternative. However, not all annuity products are the same and some perform much better than others—occasionally by as much as two to three fold. There are times when annuities make far better sense than market investments, but the reverse is also true. Important variables include such subtle things as whether the money is IRA or non-IRA, and not so subtle things such as taxes, liquidity needs, risk tolerance, inheritance concerns, etc.

Real Estate. Some people regard secondary real estate as a financial entity and sometimes that's true (your primary residence is NOT an "investment"). However, for every person who manages real estate properly and efficiently, there are far more who do not. Good vs. bad real estate ownership can involve subtle differences including the type of property, its precise, physical location ("location, location, location"), its proximity to you, the age of the property, the quality of construction of any structure, access to repair and other maintenance services, liquidity outside the real estate (Real Estate is NOT liquid), liability considerations and so forth. Most rental real estate investors find success or failure in one variable—choosing the tenant. A good tenant results in success and a bad tenant (one who fails to pay or pay timely, or damages the property or both) leads to failure even when otherwise properly managed. But real estate as an investment is unique in that it allows you to leverage your capital, depreciate the investment, and deduct your expenses. However real estate requires personal involvement and constant attention.

Insurance. Yes, insurance is a financial category, and everyone needs some form of insurance, but what type? Possible choices may include Health, Disability, Long Term Care, Property, Liability, etc. However, different carriers can quote very differently for what is seemingly the same level of coverage. Even getting multiple quotes from different carriers does not completely resolve this because unless you know *exactly what* you are being quoted (subtle differences in coverage can make huge differences in premium), price shopping for the "best quote" can lead to costly mistakes. Further, not everyone needs every type of insurance. For example, a wealthy person with no debt and no heirs (of concern) has little need for Life Insurance, but may have a need for long term care insurance, particularly if the "wealth" is not readily available to pay the high cost of care when care is needed. With limited exception, everyone needs some form of liability insurance and most "well-to-do" families should consider umbrella liability coverage. Liability insurance is the foundation of any asset protection plan.

These are but a few examples of how the "big picture" is so dependent on the "little details."

Whether legal document, financial account, or insurance policy, owning a product is a *consequence* of planning and *not* the plan itself. A product is nothing more than a tool whose purpose is to accomplish a particular goal. No tool is worthy of recommendation until *after* determining that it is needed and suitable for a particular purpose. Regardless of how many people have the same or similar needs, no product or solution is appropriate until its recommendation has followed a process of due diligence and consideration.

Hallmarks of Planning:

1. Family Dynamics: What are your goals? Dreams? Loves? Fears? What events in life (financial, relationship, spiritual, charitable, health and well-being, etc.) are important to you?
2. Time and Flexibility: When will there be significant changes in your life?
    - Planned: Starting a job, or career. Getting married. Having children. Sending your kids to college. Retiring. Etc.
    - Unplanned: Major repairs to the home. Moving. Medical issues. Death of a family member. Your death.

Life's circumstances change constantly. Good planning is not just about anticipating what you need today (when you draft the plan) but tomorrow when what you relied on today to make that plan may change.

Do-it-yourself-planning lacks the experience and foresight that a Professional can bring. Through education and training, resource and experience, Professional Planners can help people better anticipate how to address those changes. In addition, they have access to a wide array of tools not available to lay persons, and they can function in an independent capacity to facilitate transitions as they occur. Planning that focuses solely on the products: the Will or Trust, the investment portfolio, the insurance policy misses the mark because it assumes the products are the ultimate answers. They're not. Planning stems from the advice. The product is merely an extension of that advice.

Another void created by do-it-yourself planning is access to the best of the best. Many times, the most ideal solution is available only from a licensed professional. Just like a prescription medication can only be obtained with a prescription written by a medical doctor, many financial products and legal documents can only be obtained from a licensed professional. It doesn't matter how much you think you know. There is a very real set of solutions available only from professionals.

Finally, many people think they know things—especially when deluged by information on the internet, the news media, talk show media jocks, or worse, advice from friends and relatives—who heard it from someone, who heard it from… But just because something is touted in popular conversation does not make it true or appropriate for you. Marc Twain said:

"It's not what you don't know that causes the most trouble. It's what you know for certain that just ain't so."

When it comes to planning, most folks are surprised at the level of options that are available when they get good advice.

MONEY SECRET: Don't be a do-it-yourselfer. Find and take advantage of Professional Advice because…

1. You don't know as much as you think you do.
2. You don't know as much as licensed, trained professionals.
3. You don't have access to all the resources that professionals do and many of those exclusive resources are better than what's available to the masses.
4. Fixing mistakes costs far more than taking steps to avoid mistakes from the start.

But HOW do you find a good professional? Every advisor will claim to be the best of the best. Clearly that can't be true.

Step 1. Look for professional credentials. Anyone can claim to be a "financial advisor." Without professional credentials backing that claim up, it's little more than boasting.

Step 2. Interview them. Seek not only a Professional Advisor with whom you are comfortable and whose advice you trust, but also has a Fiduciary Duty to put your best interests ahead of all others, and most importantly, are openly proud of that fact.

Test them to see what their values are:

- What's the advisor's process?
- Do they start with determining your goals and then offer products to match or the other way around?

- Be cautious about anyone who is too quick to recommend products, whether financial or legal. An advisor who jumps to a product sale before completing a thorough needs analysis may be more focused on peddling that product than providing a customized solution.
- But even after a thorough fact-finder, ask HOW the recommendation will function specific to meeting those needs.
- Make sure you understand the costs (internal and external), the benefits, and the risks.
- Make sure the professional fully informs you, not just what the product (legal document or financial product is), but HOW it specifically works for you. Make sure you can actually recite back what those functional advantages are. Having something make sense when being told by a knowledgeable expert is not the same thing as knowing what it is. People hear things and then forget, or think they understand how something works but don't.
- Don't be afraid to ask for something to be explained again.
- Don't commit to something that you don't understand but don't walk away thinking you'll understand it later on your own. Keep asking until you understand—and please *ask*, don't *challenge*. For example, asking is: "*I'm sorry can you please explain _____ again.*" Challenging is: "*Well so and so says...*"
- Recognize that good planning is holistic—it combines everything: legal, investment, accounting and taxes, banking, and insurance—all working together in synergy. One hallmark of a good advisor is someone who openly works with other professionals, all for your best interest.

Step 3. Once you have found a professional who you do trust, then trust that advisor. Be respectful of his/her time, effort and expertise. Once you have been through the planning process, have been given a recommendation that you understand, follow that advice and move forward to implement whatever recommendation was offered. Otherwise, it's the case of "*If you don't want to take my advice, don't ask for it.*"

CHAPTER 2
LIABILITY INSURANCE

Foundation of Asset Protection—

In 1978, Chief Justice Warren Burger predicted "*We may well be on our way to a society overrun by hordes of lawyers, hungry as locusts, and brigades of judges in numbers never before contemplated.*" At that time, there were approximately 450,000 lawyers in the United States. Thirty-six years later, according to a 2014 article in the Boston Globe, that number surpassed 1.22 Million. Since then, the rate of newly licensed attorneys has decreased but there are still a lot of lawyers out there and many are starving for clients.

One of the easiest ways for an attorney to make money is find someone to sue. Basically, anybody can sue anyone for anything even if they did nothing wrong. At the end of the day, regardless of the merits of the claim or the judgment, being sued costs you a lot of money.

Most litigation attorneys look for deep pockets because they commonly bill on a contingency basis, meaning they get a share of the settlement *only* if they win. But because they get a large share of the settlement, the size of the claim will also be as large as possible.

Therefore, Asset Protection is far more than simply protecting financial accounts from stock market losses. It's also about having liability protection and where you invest or how much you're worth makes no difference without being protected in every area of potential liability.

Professional Liability (E&O)

Licensed professionals: doctors, lawyers, CPAs, financial professionals, etc. all carry professional liability insurance known as "Errors and Omissions" (E&O). Similarly, manufacturing and other "blue collar" employers carry Workman's Compensation Insurance. These coverages are generally required as part of the normal business practice. Depending on the nature of the profession or business, such insurance can range from nominal to prohibitively expensive.

However, some businesses have no formal liability protection requirement. Often because of the expense and a belief that they don't need it, they remain exposed. Sole proprietorships are especially vulnerable and in many cases, people don't even realize there is risk or how great that risk actually can be. For example, if a sole proprietorship business gets sued, the entirety of personal assets of the business owner may be on the hook.

One of the most surprising and risky examples is with people who own a second (or third) property that they rent out, if even to "*just friends or relatives.*" Regardless of how "casual," the act of renting property means they are in the real estate business and exposes them to full liability as a business owner. Any incident, regardless of actual fault or circumstances, can result in litigation for which the owner has no good recourse other than mount a legal defense. Regardless of the outcome, that's going to be very expensive.

Finally, it's important to understand that business liability refers to actions of *both* the business and its employees. For example, if an employer has a driver who is in an accident, not only can that driver get sued, the employer can get sued as well.

There are a number of ways a small business owner can be protected from liability. The simplest is with liability insurance from an umbrella policy. Umbrella coverage is obtained from the insurance company who insures your house or condo and car. With limited exception, the coverage is relatively inexpensive: $1 Million of liability typically costs a couple hundred dollars extra per year.

Small business owners whose businesses are organized as corporations (LLC, LLP or S-Corp) can obtain umbrella protection by having their company directly purchase the coverage. This is a tax-deductible expense. Sole proprietors can purchase the liability protection individually and deduct it as well.

Personal Liability for Individuals

Individuals with no independent business interests are still at risk for litigation. The biggest source of risk is driving a vehicle. Contrary to popular opinion, most auto insurance provides only minimal protection and drivers who opt for only what is required by law are at risk. Some states have no requirement for coverage and your own coverage may be your only protection if an underinsured driver hits you.

For example, in North Carolina (and most states), the required amount of liability insurance on an auto policy is from $30,000 to $60,000. Compare that with the average liability resulting from a serious accident of $1 Million or more.

Individual umbrella policies are obtained as an extension of your home and auto insurance. This coverage includes not only the cost associated with an unfavorable judgment, but also the cost of the defense which is not included in the limits of liability. For example, you have an accident and are at fault. The harmed party wins a $1 Million law suit. But, in addition to the judgment, you owe $150,000 in legal fees. Fortunately, you have a $1 Million umbrella policy which pays *both* the $1 Million judgment *and* the $150,000 legal fees.

So how much umbrella coverage should you have?

The typical range is from $1 to $5 Million but to determine the right ballpark, calculate your total net worth and that's how much coverage you theoretically should have. But, this introduces a double-edged sword.

On the one hand, being under-insured opens you up for risk. Note that just because you have $1 Million of protection does not mean you can't get sued for $2 Million. Because million-dollar settlements and judgments are increasingly more common, $2 Million may be the sweet spot, especially for well-to-do families. However, because the vast majority of law suits settle out long before they end up in court and because litigators seeking to maximize their share start by suing for more than you're worth, larger umbrella policies could paint a bigger target.

Thus, the correct answer of how much coverage is right depends on a host individual circumstances that can only be properly addressed by direct conversation with a licensed insurance professional. To that end, we strongly recommend finding and establishing a good working relationship with a professional insurance agent who will invest the time to learn your particular situation and customize a recommendation for you.

Mass media marketing programs boast they are convenient and can save you money. First, with insurance you get what you pay for so "saving money" is a euphemism for "minimal coverage."

Purchasing coverage over the phone or online from a representative who "hides" behind the veil of a phone bank or the internet deprives you the value of true customized advice and exposes you to risk you're unaware of until tragedy strikes. Now, you must face very bad financial news right after having to deal with very bad news physically. It's a case of adding insult to injury.

Just how real are these situations? There was a case of woman, six weeks pregnant who caused an auto accident that killed her daughter and the loss of her unborn child. She had an umbrella policy and her son-in-law was awarded an amount equal to the full value of the policy. Without that policy, the judgment would likely have been the same (juries usually do not know if insurance exists or how much is available when they render a judgment).

MONEY SECRET: Don't make any assumptions. Find a good property and casualty insurance advisor with whom you can meet face-to-face. This professional will become a central person in your life like your doctor, dentist, attorney, and CPA. Avoid the temptation of trying to save a few bucks by calling those mass marketed insurers because "*operators are standing by—call today.*" What seems cheap today may turn costly later if insurance coverage is actually needed. Even more important, with a personal agent you have one person to call; a person who knows you and can help when tragedy strikes. Good luck getting through, much less finding the same person who signed you up online or via the phone. There is no substitute for having a Personal Insurance Agent for Property and Casualty Insurance coverage.

CHAPTER 3
SOCIAL SECURITY MISTAKES

Social Security income planning is something few people do until they're close to retirement. However, good Social Security income planning should start years, if not decades before. Many factors can significantly impact the amount of one's guaranteed monthly income check and how much of that income is subjected to tax. Good planning well in advance can have a significant impact on that eventual result.

To begin with, it's necessary to dispel a common myth: Social Security is NOT going away and failing to plan for it because of that belief is one of the biggest retirement income mistakes a person can make. Another idea that leads to bad decisions is when a friend or loved one dies prior to receiving Social Security, and you take that as a sign to take your benefit as early as possible to guarantee you'll get back what you paid in.

Two factors which significantly alter the amount of Social Security income are the years of earned income prior to Full Retirement Age and the age at which Social Security is elected.

Social Security calculates the basic retirement benefit (called Primary Insurance Amount or PIA) from the best 35 years of earned income prior to full retirement age (66-67 depending on year of birth). Since most workers have their highest earnings during the last 10 or so years of employment, retiring early means entering "0's" in the columns normally reserved for the highest income numbers. Anyone who's ever looked at school grades knows how devastating even one "0" can have to the overall grade. Therefore, working at full pay, even maximum pay, up to at least Full Retirement Age can have a huge impact on the actual size of the Social Security check (although Social Security caps the allowed computational income at about $120,000 per year).

Full Retirement Age is determined by the year of birth. For people born in 1954 or earlier, Full Retirement Age is 66. People born between 1954 and 1960, it advances two months per year and for people born after 1960, Full Retirement Age is 67.

The second major determinant of Social Security income is the age at which Social Security is elected.

Technically, there are three benchmark dates in the Social Security election cycle. Full Retirement Age is the age at which the PIA is fully vested and paid as income. However, people are permitted to take their Social Security as early as age 62; widows and widowers can take at age 60. But doing so subjects the recipient to two penalties.

The first penalty is a general reduction of the PIA by 8% per year it is taken early. For example, Jim, whose Full Retirement Age is 67 has a PIA of $2000 per month, elects to start benefits at 62. His PIA will be reduced by 40% to $1200 per month. This is a lifetime reduction of 40% that cannot be adjusted later.

The second penalty occurs if the Social Security recipient continues to work (even part time) after starting Social Security benefits. If that earned income exceeds a relatively low threshold ($16,920 in 2017), Social Security docks the recipient $1 of Social Security income for every $2 earned above the threshold. For example, if Jim takes a part time job and earns $1810/month, his Social Security income will be further reduced to $1000/month (a $200 monthly reduction due to income). He is now earning one half of what he would get at full retirement age. At least this second penalty does goes away at full retirement age. This means that once you reach full retirement age, you can earn as much income as you want without reducing your Social Security payments.

Conversely, every year you delay starting Social Security through your Maximum Retirement Age (70), Social Security increases your PIA by 8% per year. Thus, in our previous example, if Jim waited until 70 before electing benefits, he would receive $2640 per month, and working after the Full Retirement Age does not reduce the Social Security benefit. Thus, if Jim took that part time job and continued to work, electing Social Security at 70, his total income now would be $4450 per month.

In addition, Social Security income actually increases with inflation and by the truest measure of inflation: the Consumer Price Index of All Urban Measures (CPI-U) which includes the standard CPI plus gas, groceries and home heating fuel. In other words, if annual inflation was 2.5%, Jim's Social Security checks would be further increased by 2.5% per year. With compounding, a bigger monthly check results in bigger increases. For example, a 2.5% increase on $3,000 = $75; while a 2.5% increase on $2,000 = $50.

Often people retire as soon as possible, justifying that they've "*worked long and hard enough*" and that they'll be able to live off Social Security and pension. This decision, however fails to consider all the available options and the factors that can influence income.

Apart from the reduced incomes just noted, such decisions fail to account for the need for more income later in retirement Inflation alone (based upon low to modest inflation rates) can double living costs over 30 years. But catastrophic increases can occur due to healthcare situations, hospitalizations, drug expenses, and especially Long-Term Care needs plus other lifestyle changes. The costs for Long Term Care are not covered by Medicare or most health insurance. Unfortunately, studies have shown that nearly half of people 65 and older will suffer a long-term care crisis during their lifetime. When these challenges become a reality, retirees must turn to their savings.

Spending Your Savings Is Not Income

Income is defined as a permanent, reliable source of money that is received every month that cannot be depleted by spending what was received yesterday. Withdrawing from a cash or investment account is spending—not income which depletes the account by that amount. Without growth necessary to replace what was taken this month, the withdrawn amount next month is a larger percentage of the total. It risks you outliving your money. This danger is compounded by the fact that life expectancies are increasing; that is, people live longer than they did before. It's been said that one of the most serious mistakes a person can make in planning their retirement income, is basing their life expectancy on a dead relative.

While many people understand the math behind taking Social Security early, they ignore the advice to delay because they do not know how to structure their income to justify waiting until maximum retirement age. This is where getting advice from a professional financial planner can make a big difference (see the discussion in Chapter 18. "Building Income Bridges").

People can go to the Social Security Administration for information but not advice. The Social Security Administration is not permitted to advise and the information provided often leads to poor decisions.

For example, in September 2016, the Government Accounting Office (GAO) published a report stating that over 50% of individuals were either given incorrect information or did not get complete information, especially on the benefits of waiting for maximum retirement age. To be fair, the Social Security Administration is overwhelmed with calls and there is only so much they can do.

The following are some generic answers to common questions. However, Social Security decisions can be very complex and because individual circumstances vary greatly, the need for consulting a professional for anything more than the most rudimentary needs cannot be overstated.

Spousal Benefit—Often, one spouse will receive a much larger benefit amount than the other. The lower earning spouse may elect the greater of his/her actual benefit or half of the larger earning spouse's benefit. The larger benefit spouse must be receiving his/her benefit for the other spouse to elect to receive half of that benefit amount. Moreover, the lower-earning spouse may take half the higher earning spouse's benefit and later elect to switch to his/her own benefit at a later date, if and when that makes sense (see File and Switch and Restricted Filing).

File and Suspend—This benefit which, for most people, ended May 1, 2016, allowed a Social Security recipient, at Full Retirement Age to file for his/her individual benefits and file for the spousal benefit (for a spouse at Full Retirement Age), then suspend his/her own benefit until age 70 for the maximum amount. It ended because it was a loophole that permitted people to get much more than their fair share.

However, File and Suspend for an individual still exists and can be used effectively in some circumstances. For example, suppose George, age 62 loses his job. He files for Social Security benefits. Then a year later, is hired back. He is earning in excess of $16,920 so not only does he no longer need the Social Security income, it would be reduced by the $1 for $2 formula. So, George voluntarily suspends his Social Security benefits. He continues to work until 70 and restarts his Social Security. His PIA benefit will increase by 8% per year plus inflation indexing, less an amount based on the one year in which he did receive benefits. Alternatively, George may repay Social Security the amount he was paid and later receive his full benefit amount as though he'd never taken the one year of income in the first place. However, it is important to note that a person is permitted only one voluntary suspension and during that suspension of benefits, he/she cannot continue receiving other benefits (such as spousal benefits) on another person's record.

File and Switch—A lower-earning spouse can claim his/her own Social Security benefits and then later switch to receive half of higher-earning spouses' rate when that spouse claims benefits (e.g., at age 70).

Restricted Filing—A Social Security recipient can make a Restricted Filing to seek half of a spouses' benefit, then later (from Full Retirement Age to 70) take the full benefit amount. At that time, the lesser earning spouse can now claim half of the spouse whose benefit was deferred. However, this does not happen automatically. A recipient must ask.

Surviving Spouse—When a higher earning spouse dies, the surviving spouse may elect to keep his/her own benefit or receive the benefit from the deceased spouse, whichever is greater. However, a widow/widower who is younger than Full Retirement Age will receive a reduced amount:

- Age 60—Full Retirement Age gets 71.5-99% of the deceased worker's basic amount
- Age 50 through 59—gets 71.5%
- Widow/widower 60 to Full Retirement Age—gets 75%
- A child under age 18 (19 if still in elementary or secondary school) or disabled—gets 75%.
- Dependent parent(s) of the deceased worker, age 62 or older:
  - One surviving parent—gets 82.5%
  - Two surviving parents—gets 75% to each parent.
- A special lump-sum death benefit amount may also be available.

Maximum Family Amount—There's a limit to the amount that family members can receive each month. The limit varies is generally about 150-180% of the basic benefit rate. If the sum of the benefits payable to family members is greater this limit, the benefits will be reduced proportionately. However, any benefits that are paid to a surviving divorced spouse based on disability or age won't count against this maximum amount.

Divorced Spouse Benefits—A divorced spouse, age 62 or older may claim benefits from an ex-spouse if the marriage lasted at least 10 years, the ex-spouse qualifies for Social Security benefits and is also at least 62. This is permitted even if the ex-spouse has not claimed his/her individual Social Security benefits. For example, Mary and John, both 62, divorce after 10 years of marriage. John continues to work and plans to defer his individual Social Security benefits until age 70. Mary, who is not working, may claim Divorced Spouse Benefits based on John's PIA even though John has not elected his own Social Security benefits. When he does, he will get the exact same amount he would without regard to Mary's benefit. If Mary later remarries, she may continue to claim a Divorced Spouse Benefit based on John. However, the rules state that remarriage before age 60 terminates the right to claim on the prior spouse's account.

Dependent Children of a Disabled or Deceased Parent are eligible for benefits if they are unmarried and:

- Younger than age 18
- Age 18-19 and a full time student (through Grade 12)
- Age 18 or older with a disability that began before age 22
- a stepchild, grandchild, step-grandchild or adopted child of a parent is disabled or retired and entitled to Social Security benefits including a parent who died after having worked—and paid into Social Security to qualify.

Disability Benefits—Traditional Social Security income is not the only form of Social Security benefit. Social Security also offers Disability Benefits to persons who are disabled and because of that disability, are unable work. But, this comes with a very big caveat. Regardless of how long that person worked before becoming disabled, if they did not work in the last 5 years prior to the disability (technically 20 of the last 40 quarters), they lose eligibility for Disability benefits under Social Security. Where this hurts the most is illustrated by the case of a woman who, after having a career, retired to raise the family and just over five years later, became disabled. She was ineligible for Disability Benefits under Social Security, even though by virtue of her disability, was qualified to receive those benefits.

Taxation on Social Security

Depending on a diverse number of factors, a person's Social Security benefits may range from being entirely tax-free up to 85% of the total amount subject to income tax. Within the instructions for completing Form 1040 (Individual Income Tax return) is a worksheet of 18 steps. The very first instructions are to add half of the total Social Security income amount to all other income. It then instructs to subtract a pre-stated amount depending on whether filing singly or joint. If the result of that subtraction is $0 or less, then none of the Social Security income is taxable. If the resulting subtraction is greater than $0, you complete the rest of the 18 steps to determine how much of the Social Security income is taxable. Obviously, the less "other" income that is reported, the less of your Social Security is taxable. What is surprising, however, is what counts as income. For example, income from Municipal Bonds, though not individually taxable, *does* count against Social Security in this calculation. In other words, while the bond interest is itself not taxable, it does potentially increase how much of your Social Security is taxed.

Good income planning is not just knowing when to start Social Security but also forward thinking to simultaneously maximize the amount of Social Security benefits and minimize the amount of "other" income which might negatively increase how much of that Social Security income is subject to income tax.

In other words, "*It's not how much you make that counts. It's how much you get to keep.*"

MONEY SECRET: Knowing how to maximize your Social Security payments based your personal situation is a key ingredient in retirement planning. Knowing your options for total income generation, not just Social Security income, can lead to much better long-term choices about Social Security election. Good Social Security planning makes for good Income Planning and that is why planning way before one starts Social Security is so critically important.

CHAPTER 4
REAL ESTATE AND PROPERTY MANAGEMENT

Real Estate can be a significant investment but knowing how to invest in real estate is as important as knowing how to buy any other investment (stocks, bonds, mutual funds, ETF's, gold, commodities, etc.). Many people think it's all about buying a property they like or can afford, renting it out and raking in the cash while growing the real value of the property. Unfortunately, this is not the experience for many and can be fraught with a lot of hidden traps.

On the other hand, many people avoid real estate because of the time, effort, and hassle involved in doing it well. But real estate can offer to those willing to put in the necessary sweat equity some advantages that make it different. First, it allows true diversification from market investments. It also allows you to leverage the money you have available to purchase a much more expensive property. In other words, you make a down-payment of (for example) 5% to 20% and borrow the balance to purchase the property. If your cash flow remains constant, the income pays the mortgage and other expenses while the property appreciates in value. Plus, there are tax advantages in that you can deduct interest paid, real estate tax, insurance premiums, upkeep expenses, plus you can depreciate the property, which taken together, normally lowers your income tax bill. Then years later, after the loan is paid in full, you own the property outright and your net cash flow increases (because your expenses reduced). Also, once the loan is paid, the cash flow can be more reliable and may generate more income (per dollar invested) than traditional market investments. But of course, there are risks. Unexpected expenses for repairs or maintenance can crop up at any time, and seemingly occur at the most inconvenient time when you don't have the cash available to pay for it. In addition, one bad tenant can destroy what was otherwise a good investment and natural disasters such as hurricanes, tornadoes, and floods can destroy your property or make your property uninhabitable. Even though adequate insurance will repair or replace the damaged structure itself, it will not pay you for the lost rent. Also, other factors out of your control, such as a new road, a new landfill, zoning changes, new commercial/industrial neighbors, or just bad neighbors in general, can reduce values and make selling the property at a profit impossible. Just as with other investments, the more you know before starting, the better your chances of success are. Once again, getting the best advice possible about purchasing and maintaining real estate, as well as properly managing property, will increase your opportunity for success with real estate.

Some myths about real estate as an investment:

1. The equity in your home is <u>not</u> an investment. Despite how much your personal residence appreciates in value, it may be a valuable asset, but it is not an investment. The value in your home is not something you can simply access other than through a home equity line of credit or second mortgage, but these options are limited and create debt. In fact, this limitation is why standard financial planning questionnaires specifically exclude your primary residence in your net worth calculation.

2. With limited exceptions, personal vacation properties, vacant lots, and some farms are not investment properties. Often, they do not generate profits and cannot be sold easily at a profit and even when they can be sold, they are long-term propositions. Real estate of any

kind is not considered "liquid." You can't convert it to cash quickly. More often than not, other than personal enjoyment, secondary properties are more of a liability than an asset: each year you must pay property taxes, insurance, and upkeep costs, with little or no income from the property.

3. Unless you're a licensed contractor (and licensed realtor), buying houses to fix up and flip is not advised. The laws surrounding both construction and professional real estate sales are complex and without professional training and expertise in both areas you can be exposed to a host of problems (legal and otherwise) that could end up costing you more than the property is worth.
4. Contrary to popular belief, Real Estate values do *not* always rise. In fact, the Case-Shiller Index of Home Prices from 1891 through 2017 has shown virtually no net change in home value. Note that "value" refers to the cost of a house relative to the purchasing power of a dollar. It is not the same as "price." In fact, this misassumption was one of the fundamental mistakes that gave rise to the home mortgage collapse of 2007, precipitating the Great Recession.
5. Real estate is not liquid. It is not possible to sell real estate on a moment's notice. Even if a property has a buyer before it goes on the market, there are a number required legal steps for the sale to be completed and the property's equity to end up in your bank account.

Financially, Real Estate (other than a primary residence or secondary property for personal enjoyment), falls into two broad categories: investment and business. Real estate investment occurs when the owner sells a property for profit over purchase. Real estate business refers to the generation of income through rent. It is possible to own real estate for both purposes but in those cases, the variables (and cautions) for each separately apply.

REAL ESTATE AS AN INVESTMENT

Selecting investment properties to sell for net profit ("flipping") requires several points of consideration:

- **Location, Location, Location.** A property in a high valued, growing area has a much better chance of being sold quickly and for a profit than one in an economically depressed or over-valued area.
- **Taxes, insurance, upkeep and HOA dues.** Depending on location, these (and other) expenses can significantly impact the net profitability of the property.
- **Quality of construction.** Not all houses are built equally. A property that is constructed with low grade materials and shoddy workmanship will never be as valuable as one that is well built. Unfortunately, it is difficult if not impossible for the average real estate purchaser to look behind the walls to see what really went on in the construction. A good home inspector can help with this but at best a home inspection is a snapshot in time.
- **Age and condition.** A property that is between 10 and 15 years old is rapidly approaching the time when major repairs will be needed: new roof, new heating/AC unit, garage door openers, paint, etc. A property that is much older may be a better opportunity and may be much worse, depending what repairs have already been done. Again, a good home inspection can help but is not a guarantee. The only time in a property's life when everything is new is when the property itself is new, and new houses are seldom great deals to buy and flip.
- **Distressed Property vs. Distressed Seller**. One popular strategy to finding and flipping homes is to look for properties in foreclosure. On the surface, this might seem a viable direction. However, for the most part, someone who has just lost a house to non-payment (or otherwise), is not going to have been the best caretaker of the property. Purchasing a property in foreclosure because it is inexpensive may also include purchasing a host of serious problems from property neglect.

RENTAL PROPERTY

More common than flipping properties is property rental. Here too, many of the considerations are the same as with property flipping:

Location, Location, Location. Where do you want your property: Rural, Suburban, City? Each location has advantages and disadvantages. Ideally seek a property that will be rented without turnover and by people who will take care of the property as if they owned it (Note: people seldom care for rental properties as much as when they own; some don't take care of properties they do own).

Property diversification. Owning more than one rental property requires some level of diversification not unlike investment diversification. Ideally, different homes should be different types of structures: different construction styles, different square footage, different price points, etc.

For example, a high-tech employer expands. They recruit and hire 50 top engineers. Also, a manufacturer opens a new plant and brings in 100 blue collar workers to run the plant. Both sets of new employees will need properties, but they'll want very different houses in very different neighborhoods.

Property Proximity. A rental property that's a couple miles from where you live is far easier to monitor than one located in another county or state. With property rental, out-of-sight is definitely out-of-mind and that can lead to small problems growing into major ones before you know it.

Buy as much as possible. A four-bedroom house will rent to a family seeking either three or four bedrooms, but a three bedroom house will not rent to someone seeking four.

Unwitting mistakes. Sometimes people innocently violate the law with things they do (or don't do). Consider the following examples:

1. A man buys a condo at a resort location. The property is fully managed by the condo association and it rents phenomenally well. The man wants to sell it, so he advertises how much the property has appreciated in value and how well it has rented. To make this point, he reports "*Over the last five years, the property returned an average of 7% per year.*" The man is now in violation of the Federal Securities Act of 1933 and potentially subject to both civil and criminal action.

He offered the property for sale as an investment which, without undergoing a lengthy and very expensive process of registration with the SEC (US Securities and Exchange Commission), is a violation of federal securities law. While most people who make this mistake don't get "caught," those who do, seriously regret it.

2. A man owns a three-bedroom house to be rented. A family shows up seeking to move in. They seem to be a large family with a lot of kids, so the man asks: "*How many children do you have who will live here?*" He has just violated Federal Fair Housing Law.

   Similarly, advertising things such as "*Christian-friendly*" or "*Italian-American discount*" or "*no pets*" (including service and comfort animals), or "*no wheelchairs*" (because the house is multi-level without elevators) or "*women on the top floor only*" (for personal safety) are all violations of Fair Housing Law.

   In fact, there are seven areas in which discrimination is forbidden: religion, race, familial status, nationality, handicap status, age and sex. Regardless of how well intended or innocent, a first violation of Fair Housing Law carries a $10,000 fine.

PROPERTY MANAGEMENT

A property manager is a person (or business) in charge of handling the day-to-day tasks associated with property rental. Property managers find the tenants, do the background checks, maintain the property, collect the rent, etc. While many property owners recognize that a professional property manager can perform these tasks, they remain resistant to employing them because "*it costs money.*" They feel they can do as good a job without giving up revenue. Unfortunately, this is generally not true.

First of all, professional property managers have spent a lifetime learning what they know. They are licensed and manage properties every single day as a primary business, not a "sideline" or hobby job.

Second, they are better equipped to find prospective tenants, properly vet them, maintain the property, collect the rent and keep the property rented. In the long run, these advantages mean more revenue for the landlord, not less.

Consider the following:

1. Prospective tenants have changed how they search for properties to rent. They no longer drive around looking for yard signs. Instead, they search the internet. Without a "Properties for Rent" website that does not pop up on the first or maybe second search page, it might as well not exist. For example, a recent Google Search of "Rental Properties" for a large city (population 1 Million) returned 809 000 hits. At 17 listings per page, that's 47,589 pages to sort through.
2. A professional property manager can screen prospective renters for credit scores, criminal history and eviction history. These cannot be manipulated or faked. Merely asking for references such as prior landlord, etc. can result in false information. People routinely list their best friend's phone number, etc. as reference or previous landlord to conceal an undesirable past.
3. Professional property managers keep the property owner safe from violations of Fair Housing Law and other unwitting liabilities. Not only are they knowledgeable and licensed so those mistakes are avoided, they keep the property owner at arm's length. Thus, if a mistake is made, it's on the property manager, not the property owner.
4. Efficient property maintenance. Houses have things go wrong that need repair. Renters can be very unforgiving when something is broken that they feel the landlord should fix. But without ongoing access to regular repair contractors, a landlord will face hiring the first repairman willing to visit the property, or send a friend, relative or neighbor. Apart from the uncertainty of getting the repair completed in a timely fashion, they risk sending someone who is uninsured and not bonded. Conversely, they may be forced to hire a repairman as an "emergency visit" and pay a premium charge or face telling the tenant to wait (weeks if not months) for the repair to be completed. Professional property managers have repair contractors who give them priority and larger ones have those workers on staff.

5. Collection of rents and management of security deposit. Not all tenants are diligent about paying their rent on time, if at all. Chasing after delinquent renters can be challenging and may require resources such as collections agencies, etc. One of the common protections is the collection of a security deposit but how these moneys are handled after being collected has legal implications. For example, security deposits cannot legally be comingled with personal funds. So, if you don't have a separate account just to hold the security deposits, you may be in violation of law.
6. Eviction. From time-to-time, it is necessary to evict a tenant. Unfortunately, there are legal issues associated with this that can be tricky to navigate. For example, how long must you wait before beginning the eviction process? Are you required to give advance notice? What happens if the tenant offers to make a partial rent payment? Not knowing the correct answers, and in advance of getting asked the question, puts you at risk of violation of law.

MONEY SECRET: Property ownership and rental can be lucrative as either income or investment and can function as an excellent portfolio diversifier. However, navigating the myriad of laws and efficiently managing the day-to-day operations can be tricky. The use of a professional property manager for rent and competent realtor for sales can make all the difference in the world. Not only do they perform the "heavy lifting" of the day-to-day work, but they are generally better equipped to get more money out of the property through improved efficiency, minimizing innocent mistakes and generally negotiate better than what the average "civilian" does. However, it's important to vet the property manager or realtor as well. Look at their website. Visit and interview them. Ask about their size, reach, capabilities and track record. Make sure that the professional you hire is truly the best you can find. Then, when you do, put the ball in their hands and let them do what they do best.

CHAPTER 5
SENIOR HEALTH INSURANCE

Whether we like it or not, everyone ages and at that "magical" age of 65, most Americans become eligible for the federal health insurance program known as Medicare.

Medicare started in July 1965 to provide medical insurance for people who are 65 or older, and certain younger people with disabilities or with End-Stage Renal Disease. Original Medicare includes two parts, A and B.

Medicare Part A (Hospital Insurance) covers inpatient hospital stays, limited days of care in a skilled nursing facility, hospice care, and some home health care under a doctor's supervision.

Medicare Part B (Medical Insurance) covers certain doctors' services, outpatient care, medical supplies, and preventive services.

For most people, Medicare Part A charges no premium while Part B does. In addition, neither is comprehensive so a senior covered by only Medicare Parts A and B, assumes significant financial exposure.

Starting in the early 1980's, private insurers were able to offer Medicare supplement plans, also known as "Medigap" plans. Obtained from private insurance companies, these policies fill in many of the holes in traditional Medicare A and B coverage.

In 1997, Congress added Medicare Part C, a privatized substitute for traditional Medicare called "Medicare Advantage." These plans actually take you off traditional Medicare and substitute a private insurance policy as your "Medicare." However, a person who elects a Medicare Advantage Plan is later permitted to switch back to traditional Medicare, subject to certain enrollment windows.

In 2006, Congress added Medicare Part D which specifically covers prescription drugs.

The alphabet soup of senior health insurance is complex and often mysterious to seniors who must make important choices that could impact the rest of their lives.

Medicare Part A

Most people don't pay any premium for Part A because they paid Medicare taxes while working. As of 2017, people who did not earn premium-free Part A will pay up to $413 per month for Part A.

Part A covers inpatient hospital stays, hospice care, limited Skilled Nursing Care and some Home Health Care.

In 2017, an in-hospital Medicare recipient was responsible for:

- $1,316 deductible per benefit period
- $329 daily copay after the first 60 days (which are free) up to 90 days of coverage for each benefit period.
- After 90 days of coverage, the daily co-pay increases to $658 and applies against a lifetime maximum of 60 "reserve benefit days."
- Anything beyond these limits is 100% the responsibility of the patient.

For Skilled Nursing Facility Care,

- Up to 20 days are fully covered, after three nights being "admitted" in a hospital, then
- $164.50 daily copay for days 21-100 of each benefit period, then
- 100% the patient's responsibility.
- Without being "admitted" (observation status does not count) for at

least 3 nights, there is no coverage.

- This benefit is primarily for rehabilitation; each day must be medically required.

Medicare Part B

Part B covers doctors and requires a premium. Of critical importance is that even though a person is in the hospital, doctor visits are covered under Part B, not A. In other words, Part A is facility care; Part B is treatment care.

It is possible to opt out of Part B, but doing invites very substantial risk because the more expensive component of medical care is treatment, not facility cost. Also, not electing Part B may mean no access to coverage in the future, even if you decide to "change your mind." It is simply not possible to "suddenly" decide to add Medicare Part B. One must wait for an open enrollment period, apply and then even after being accepted, wait until coverage begins in the following year. More important, enrolling during the initial enrollment period generates a substantial penalty when you do enroll. That penalty continues for life and may be more than you can afford to pay.

As of 2017, Part B covers 80% of the bills less an annual deductible of $183. The premium structure of Part B is variable based on income, but most seniors pay $120 to $134 monthly. Higher income individuals can pay $300 monthly or more, based upon your previous year income tax return.

Medicare Supplement (Medigap) Coverage

To cover the large co-pays, deductibles, and other gaps in traditional Medicare A and B coverage, an individual can elect to purchase a Medicare Supplement Policy. Medicare Supplement Plans are standardized and designated by a letter. Each lettered plan refers to a standardized different plan, some with more benefits than others and each with different premium structures. These policies are offered by private insurance companies for a premium who, while not allowed to alter the internal benefits of the plan, they are permitted to set their own premium schedules. When applying during the initial Medicare enrollment period, no medical background check is required. But if not purchased at the time of initial Medicare qualification (or following termination of other credible coverage), these plans may include medical underwriting and acceptance.

Medicare Part C (Medicare Advantage Plans)

These are private replacement plans for traditional Medicare offered by insurance companies. The insurance company contracts with Medicare to provide the equivalent of Part A and Part B benefits plus equivalent Medigap coverage. The most attractive component of Medicare Advantage plans is that they bundle coverage into a single comprehensive plan leaving only small copays and deductibles to meet and in some cases, actually offer more coverage than traditional Medicare plus Supplement. As such, an insured need only carry one insurance card and everything is covered. In addition, some Medicare Advantage plans require no premium other than continuing to pay the Medicare Part B premium. In other words, they can eliminate the added premium associated with a Medigap plan. However, most Medicare Advantage plans operate through networks of preferred providers that are designated county-by-county. Seeking care outside the network may result in substantial out-of-pocket cost, although emergency care is almost invariably covered as in-network. The patchwork nature of these plans also means that while some regions offer very good coverage through Medicare Advantage, others are virtually without coverage. And, if you elect a Medicare Advantage plan and your preferred provider is not part of or leaves the network, you may be stuck until the next open enrollment period before being able to switch back, plus, purchasing a Medicare Supplement Plan may be subject to medical underwriting. Thus, the decision to use Medicare Advantage is very dependent on the geographic region in which you live as well as ensuring that your preferred doctors and hospitals participate with the plan. Finally, if you elect a Medicare Advantage Plan, it is important to review your plan annually as plans can change from year to year.

Medicare Part D (prescription drug coverage)

Traditional Medicare has never offered prescription drug coverage. Medicare Part D adds prescription drug coverage to both Original Medicare and Medicare Advantage plans. There is a premium for these plans after which prescription drugs are covered with co-pays that vary based on what "tier" the drug is considered. Commonly, there are four tiers including generic drugs (Tier 1), preferred name brand drugs (Tier 2), non-preferred name brand drugs (Tier 3) and "specialty" drugs (Tier 4). Generally, the higher the tier, the larger the co-pay will be.

Sometimes people mistakenly assume that "*I don't take any medication, so I don't need a prescription drug plan*" and don't sign up when eligible. But if you don't enroll and then suddenly get sick, you cannot opt in until the next Annual Election Period and now you are responsible for 100% of your prescription drug costs until coverage begins. As with Part B, not enrolling in Part D during your initial eligibility window imposes a lifetime late enrollment penalty when you do enroll.

Medicare Enrollment Rules

Enrollment in Original Medicare and Medicare Part D is required and failure to do so can result in substantial penalties.

The Initial Enrollment Period is a person's birth month in the year they turn 65, plus the three months before and three months after; in other words, a seven month window. Failure to enroll within that window results in a 10% annual penalty for every year delayed. And that penalty continues for life. Similarly, failure to enroll in Medicare Part D during the Initial Enrollment Period results in a penalty of 1% per month for every month after the initial enrollment period. That penalty also continues for life.

In addition, once the Initial Enrollment Period is missed, the next possible opportunity to enroll is during the Annual Election Period (AEP) which extends from October 15 through December 7. However, the coverage does not start right away. Thus, if you miss the initial enrollment you could find yourself without coverage for the better part of a year, or more.

If you turn 65 but are covered by a "qualified" employer's plan, including your spouses' plan (called "credible coverage"), you still must enroll for Medicare Parts A and B even if your regular insurance plan will continue (an employer plan must have a least 20 employees in their plan for this to count). However, as long as you are working with "credible coverage," you may defer payment of your Medicare Part B premium. However, what constitutes "credible coverage" may be tricky. Therefore, don't assume, ask your insurer. Similarly, if that private insurance plan includes prescription drug coverage, enrollment in Medicare Part D may also be deferred without penalty until your coverage on that private plan ends. However, if you turn 65 and are covered by COBRA from a former employer, you may or may not be protected from the penalties imposed for late enrollment although you will have up to 8 months to enroll. Ask the insurer or call Medicare to verify your individual situation.

Changing coverage

Once a plan is chosen you may change to a different plan only at certain times of the year. For example, you may switch from Original Medicare to Medicare Advantage or from one Medicare Advantage Plan to another only during the open enrollment period (October 15 through December 7) every year. In addition, you may switch from Medicare Advantage to original Medicare between January 1 and February 14. Unfortunately, all too often, a person who lives in a strong Medicare Advantage coverage area will persuade friends or relatives who live in a poor coverage area to switch. Then when they discover the mistake, it's too late to change back until the next time the AEP rolls around. In the meantime, that person is functionally without coverage.

Medicare Part B Premiums

Regardless of whether a person elects Original Medicare or Medicare Advantage, they must pay the Part B Premium. This amount can vary dramatically depending on several factors, most notably income. This income surcharge is called IRMA.

For example, in 2017, the standard Part B premium was $134 per month for a single or married filing separate annual tax return of $85,000 or for married filing joint of $170,000. The following chart illustrates the premium step-ups:

File Individually	File Joint	File Married & Separated	Monthy Premium
$85,000 or less	$170,000 or less	$85,000 or less	$134.00
above $85,000 up to $107,000	above $170,000 up to $214,000	N/A	$187.50
above $107,000 up to $160,000	above $214,000 up to $320,000	N/A	$267.90
above $160,000 up to $214,000	above $320,000 up to $428,000	above $85,000 up to $129,000	$348.30
above $214,000	above $428,000	above $129,000	$428.60

Medicare Part D Premiums

Similarly, the Part D premium depends on income and tax filing status. In 2017, the national base plan premium was $35.63 but based on income, surcharges (IRMA) may be applied.

File Individually	File Joint	File Married & Separated	Monthy Premium
$85,000 or less	$170,000 or less	$85,000 or less	Plan Premium
above $85,000 up to $107,000	above $170,000 up to $214,000	N/A	$13.30 plus Plan Premium
above $107,000 up to $160,000	above $214,000 up to $320,000	N/A	$34.20 plus Plan Premium
above $160,000 up to $214,000	above $320,000 up to $428,000	above $85,000 up to $129,000	$55.20 plus Plan Premium
above $214,000	above $428,000	above $129,000	$76.20 plus Plan Premium

Getting Advice

Every state has a Senior Health Insurance Information Program (SHIIP) with counselors available through your state's department of insurance.

Usually, there is an excellent website for SHIIP with comparative date on each plan and policy found on the department of insurance website. Plus, the counselors offer free objective information on a wide array of topics in this arena. However, they cannot make specific recommendations for you nor can they promote one company or product over another.

MONEY SECRET: Health issues are the Number 1 cause of financial distress in retirement. Being adequately protected from the cost of medical care is among the most important aspects of retirement planning. Original Medicare is obtained directly through the Social Security Administration office. Anyone privately seeking to "sign you up" is selling something. However, obtaining supplemental insurance requires a fully licensed insurance agent and getting a Medicare Advantage plan requires working with a licensed agent who is also certified by CMS (Centers for Medicare and Medicaid Services) to offer those plans.

The complexity of how all the various Medicare plans work, the costs involved, and your available choices is substantial. No one should take advice from anyone who is not licensed and certified. Finally, planning ahead, including learning the various available options in your area, factoring your personal health issues, and then making one choice vs. another can be mind-blowing, but your willingness to plan for Medicare will ensure the best possible outcome.

CHAPTER 6
CAR & HOME INSURANCE

Turn on the TV or go to the movies and you're deluged with car insurance ads that either promise to save you money by switching or suggest that only they will adequately insure you or they alone give you extra services to take care of your family. Most people recognize these claims as marketing hype, but are not sure where the truth stops and the hype begins.

CAR INSURANCE: What is the truth?

1. Insurance is regulated by the states and while there is general consistency from state-to-state, individual differences do exist. Most states require a minimum amount of liability coverage (for harm or damage that you might do others), but some states have no requirement. Within a state, all base auto insurance policies are the same. The policy terms and definitions are the same from one company to the next. The only difference in policies is the coverages that you select. In other words, the companies are competing on two things—price and service. Most insurers offer a choice of basic benefit packages and premium packages with better coverage. Additional coverage items may also be purchased as riders. Depending on individual circumstances, the premium packages and riders may or may not be worth the added expense.

2. Most carriers offer discounted rates for new customers, commonly around 15% (which is why so many auto ads tout "*we'll save your 15% or more.*" But after the first year, those "low introductory rates" rise and the increased premiums effectively compensate the insurance company for the incentive discount. Fundamentally, insurance companies understand that most people won't switch after the rates go up and that data is factored into the initial pricing. Insurance companies, if nothing else, are experts at statistics and long-term projections. They never give something away without an expectancy to get it back later. Frankly, unless you are willing to change your insurance carrier every 2 to 3 years you will not save a lot over time.
3. Some companies boast benefits such as "Accident Forgiveness" and "New Car Replacement." These are supplemental benefits that are sold for additional premium and are not exactly what people believe from the ads. While these riders may be of value, be careful about broad assumptions. For example:
    a. **Accident Forgiveness**—is a provision that if you get into an at-fault accident, and it's your first in the last three years, the insurance company won't report it as an accident claim. Such reports result in "points" being stacked against your driving record. Generally, you must have a clean driving record to get the rider.
    b. **New Car Replacement**—The subliminal message of the advertisement is you will receive a brand-new car if your car is totaled. This assumption is patently false. When you buy a new vehicle and drive it off the lot, it's no longer "new" and is devalued accordingly. Insurance companies use third party vendors (called adjustors) to value a wrecked car. If you purchased a New Car Replacement rider, your compensation will typically be enough to purchase a car one year younger or with 15,000 fewer miles than your wrecked one—after you pay your plan deductible. Finally, New Car Replacement riders are not available in all states.
    c. **GAP Insurance**—is an alternative to "New Car Replacement." It is especially valuable for cars being purchased through financing.

Suppose you buy a car for $25,000 with $0 down and 0% interest. Essentially, you owe $25,000 on the car. To begin with, the car in such circumstances did not actually cost $25,000. The actual retail cost of the car is less, let's say $23,000, because the interest on the loan is built into the "purchase price" (which is why the dealer said "0% interest). If you wreck the car while driving it off the lot, at best, the car's replacement value is just $23,000—but you still owe $25,000. Now, you're now "upside down" by $2000. GAP Insurance covers the difference between the actual cash value of a vehicle and the balance you still owe through financing.

Gap Insurance is sold by financing companies, not insurance companies and is becoming increasingly harder to find. In most cases, GAP Insurance is not expensive but that can vary tremendously. Some cars are much more expensive than others and GAP Insurance on those can be much more. However, GAP policies are negotiable at the time of purchase. Talk to your insurance professional about this type coverage *before* car and car finance shopping.

4. Financially, the cost of insurance, taxes, fees—everything should be dove-tailed into the total purchase budget for a car. A vehicle that costs $25,000 to purchase and subsequently costs an additional $1500/year for taxes and insurance, if held for 5 years, actually cost $32,500.

What's Covered?

Auto policies include several basic components some are mandated by states departments of insurance, some are not.

Collision—This is coverage for damage to *your* car due to an accident involving another vehicle or a fixed object (guard rail, telephone pole, tree, etc.).

Comprehensive (Comp)—This is for any damage other than a collision. It may include fire, theft, flood, vandalism, riots, hail, rocks into the windshield and animal collisions. Note, if you hit a tree, that's covered by Collision. If you hit a deer, that's covered by Comprehensive. If you have a policy that lacks comprehensive coverage, that deer strike is not covered.

Liability Coverage—This is coverage for bodily injury and personal property due to accidents for which you are legally liable (your fault). Liability coverage pays for bodily injury, including medical expenses and personal injuries, and for property damage to the other party (but not you).

Medical Payments—This is coverage for medical treatment for injuries, whether to yourself or others, due to a collision. It is in addition to coverage by your health insurance coverage and is in addition to receiving a settlement for medical expenses from another driver under their liability coverage if they were at fault. Unfortunately, many insurance agents downplay this coverage to reduce your premium by a few dollars. Don't be fooled. You should consider getting the maximum coverage available because it is the least expensive medical insurance you can buy, particularly when it is most needed. It is one area of optional coverage you should take, particularly if you're a senior on Medicare because Medicare requires a pay-back from a liability claim for any expense covered by Medicare. This Medicare pay-back will significantly reduce the amount of money you receive due to your injuries from that settlement while the Medical Payments coverage is paid directly to you from your insurance policy regardless of whether there is a claim against someone else. This money is not subject to a Medicare pay-back.

Personal Injury Protection (PIP)—This is similar to Medical Payments coverage but covers a wider range of costs. It can help pay for medical and rehabilitation expenses, work loss, funeral costs, and even replacement services. Like Medical Payments coverage, it pays for expenses when you need them the most, and is less expensive than other forms of similar coverage.

Uninsured/Underinsured Motorist—This provides coverage if the other (at fault) party is not fully insured. Despite the requirement to have auto insurance to legally operate a motor vehicle, an estimated 1 in 8 drivers are either uninsured or inadequately insured. Your own insurance provides this coverage up to the limits of your own coverage. Hence, when you purchase liability coverage to protect others, you are also protecting yourself from others who don't carry enough insurance. Well-to-do families in particular should maximize their liability protection with uninsured and underinsured motorist coverage.

Single ownership/joint ownership—Married couples often purchase a vehicle and put the title in both names. This may have some negative consequences for your insurance protection, but if you use joint ownership, consider using Joint Ownership with Rights of Survivorship. This may require an additional form to fill out, but makes title transfer far easier, faster, and cheaper for the survivor when one dies. However, a better option is for the principal driver of the vehicle to be the sole owner. This is for insurance reasons. If the driver is negligent and injures the passenger spouse, the injured spouse can recover against the owner's insurance policy—provided the passenger does not own (co-own) the vehicle. This is true even if the passenger spouse owns another vehicle on the same insurance policy—and you can still get your multi-car discounts.

HOMEOWNER'S INSURANCE

In contrast to the plethora of car insurance ads, one seldom hears about homeowner's insurance. This is a bit surprising in that for most people, a home is the largest single asset they possess. Car and home insurance are sold by the same companies and in most cases, are bundled. In other words, you don't buy your car insurance from one company and your home insurance from another. More to the point, you wouldn't want to. Insurers understand that a person who owns two policies is at lower risk of filing claims on both than if one or the other were insured separately. In addition, umbrella policies are only attached to these base coverages not to mention that insuring separately would be a lot more expensive than insuring as a bundle.

What's Covered?

Most standard homeowner's policies include four areas of coverage:

Structure—This coverage pays to repair or rebuild a home if damaged or destroyed by fire, hurricane, tornado, hail, lightning or other disasters *listed in the policy*. Most policies include coverage for detached structures such as a garage, tool shed or gazebo. Generally the coverage is up to a stated limit (e.g., 10% of the insured value of the basic structure). Most policies require a separate policy or rider for "wind and hail" and/or for "flood," depending on the location of the property.

Standard Homeowner's coverage does *NOT* pay for:

- Floods (including mudflows)
- Ground Movement (earthquakes, sink holes, etc.)
- Mold and mildew
- Wear and Tear (including burst pipes if not by freezing—the damage the water does is covered, but repairing the pipes themselves may not be).
- Infestations including termites
- Government Actions
- Dangerous/aggressive dogs
- Emotional support (pain and suffering due to a loss)
- Sewer back-ups
- Backyard Swimming Pool and Trampoline accidents (more frequent than commonly assumed)
- Acts of terrorism, war, nuclear accidents
- Any item specifically cited as not being covered (read the policy)

Personal belongings—Covers damage or loss of furniture, clothes, sports equipment and other personal items if due to insured events listed under "Structure." Generally, personal belongings coverage is set at 50-70% percent of the insured value of the structure.

Personal belongings coverage also includes items stored off-premises meaning covered anywhere in the world. Some policies impose upper limits on the amount of coverage (e.g., 10%) and may also include limited coverage for other losses such as up to $500 on unauthorized credit card use.

Expensive items such as art, jewelry, collectibles, furs, coin collections, optical equipment, silverware, etc. may be covered to stated limits (not particularly high) but these items are better covered through special personal property endorsements (riders) that specifically list the item(s). Coverage is then based on an officially appraised value of each item separately.

Trees, plants, shrubs and other ornamental aspects of landscaping are commonly covered but generally to a limit of $500 per item, excluding damage by wind or disease.

Liability—This provides protection against lawsuits for bodily injury or property damage caused by fault or negligence of persons affiliated with the property as well and for damage caused to others by your pets. For example, if your dog ruins a neighbor's expensive rug, it's covered but if it's your rug, you're not (unless the rug is separately insured through a separate endorsement).

However, the limits of liability on standard policies are low (e.g., $100,000). This is where having a separate umbrella policy ($1-5 Million) is a good idea.

Additional Living Expenses (ALE)—This pays for the additional cost of living away from home resulting from damage or destruction of the home. It covers hotel bills, restaurant meals, and other costs, that are over and above usual living expenses, incurred while a home is being repaired or rebuilt.

ALE coverage does have limits that may include both monetary and time limitations. To an extent, these limits are adjustable based on the amount of coverage that is purchased. This is another area of discussion with an insurance professional.

RENTER'S COVERAGE (TENANT POLICY)

People who rent rather than own have access to essentially identical coverage as home owners except their coverage excludes Structure. College students are also eligible for a simplified form of renter's insurance as a rider on a basic home owner's (or renter's) insurance policy.

FLOOD INSURANCE

Regular homeowner's policies do *not* cover damage from environmental water (flooding caused by rising creeks, rivers, lakes, encroachment by the ocean, or damage caused by rain or snow including mud slides. This level of coverage is only available from policies issued by the National Flood Insurance Program (NFIP) which can be obtained through individual insurance companies. Flood coverage covers structural damage and damage to contents directly caused by water. If the flood water carries large objects (e.g., trees, rocks, etc.) that end up on the property and must be removed, that is not covered. If your home is at-risk for these possibilities, adding flood insurance can protect your investment. (If you have a mortgage, often your lender will require this coverage to obtain your loan.)

MONEY SECRET: Property and Casualty Insurance (home car, liability) is complex. Without professional advice, it's easy to be both inadequately insured in some important areas while being over insured in others. Having a good agent that you personally know and trust, who can give *you* individualized advice is the best way to ensure that you have the right amount of coverage for the least amount of premium. Avoid doing business with any insurer that offers coverage by "hidden" agents (policies obtained over the phone or online).

CHAPTER 7
LIFE INSURANCE PLANNING

Basics

At its most basic, life insurance is a contract with an insurance company where one or more designated beneficiaries receive a cash payment when the insured person dies. However, life insurance can be that or much more, depending on the kind of life insurance, how it's structured, how it's owned and the purpose for the policy.

Understanding Insurable Need

"Insurable Need" means the reason for owning a life insurance policy and the reason for a specified amount of insurance. There are two distinct ways this concept is applied.

1. Increasingly, insurance companies scrutinize life insurance applications for insurable need. Called "Insurable Interest," life insurance applications are underwritten not just for age and medical factors, but also financial factors to ensure that there is a justifiable financial reason for owning the policy, especially policy size. Generally, a person cannot purchase an insurance policy for more than their net worth or ten times their annual income. However, applications that stay within allowable limits are rarely rejected for reasons of Insurable Interest. Insurable interest also means that the insurance applicant

must have a legitimate relationship with the insured—Parent, Spouse, Child, Grandchild, Business Partner, Employer. You can't purchase a new policy on a person with whom you have no relationship.

2. Insurable Need also applies to the planning aspect of selecting the right kind of life insurance policy and determining the correct amount of coverage. Although not a part of formal company underwriting, Insurable Need analysis is an important step in deciding what type of insurance to get, how much benefit is appropriate and whether the type of insurance is suitable. For example, if someone buys a life insurance policy and names a parent as the policy's only beneficiary, it's a good bet they bought the policy on recommendation without considering if there was a legitimate insurable need for the coverage. When good insurance need planning is performed, Insurable Interest is simultaneously served.

Temporary vs. Permanent Coverage

Life Insurance policies may be structured as temporary (Term) or Permanent (Cash Value).

Term Insurance is the cheapest form of life insurance because it is designed to insure for a specific time and not beyond. For example, a 20 Year Term policy will exist for exactly 240 months after which, the coverage goes away. According to a 1993 study at Penn State, only about 1% of term policies ever paid a claim. This is because most people either outlive their policies or discontinue them before the end of the term. According to the study, 90% of the time policies are discontinued before the term expires. Sometimes the need for the policy goes away (the mortgage is paid, the kids grow up, etc.) and sometimes the premium increases to an "unreasonable" amount or an insureds cost of living increased relative to income and something had to go.

Pricing Term Insurance—Term insurance is pure insurance and the premium charged is based on two calculations: The cost of insurance (COI) and the excess above COI that pays the insurance company.

Cost of Insurance is simply the likelihood of a death claim the company must pay out compared to the premium that is paid in. For example, assume 1000 policy owners, each with $100,000 of insurance. If this year, only one of those people (statistically) is expected to die, the cost of insurance is $100 ($100,000 paid out divided by 1000 insureds). If five years from now, five deaths per year are expected, then the cost of insurance for that year has increased to $500 and so forth. The premium calculation is then based on the average cost of insurance for all years those 1000 people are to be insured. That amount, of course is increased by an amount necessary to pay the insurance company, its employees, agents, etc. for being able to provide the insurance in the first place.

Administrative Expenses covers insurance company operations, including profit margins. These finances are carefully regulated by each state's department of insurance. The occasionally expressed notion that insurance companies are heartless, greedy, run-away gougers is simply not correct. "Heartless" in some cases may be a fair accusation, but premiums are priced according to formal guidelines and you get what you pay for.

Term Life is most appropriately used when protecting from a financial harm that exists only to a specified future date beyond which that need no longer exists (or is diminished). For example, a couple with one spouse being a stay-at-home parent may require term insurance on the primary income earner's life until the kids are through school and on their own. The insurable amount should be established such that if the income-earner dies tomorrow, the death benefit would replace that working spouse's income long enough for the surviving spouse to carry on until the income need no longer exists. Properly identifying all the variables, including the term (number of years the policy lasts), the face amount (how big the policy is) and other considerations are a matter of professional insurance planning. Randomly picking an arbitrary term and amount because they "seem right" can result in a policy either being woefully inadequate or far more than needed.

Mortgage Protection is a commonly sold version of Term. For the sales agent, it's an emotional sale and easy pitch: "*Protect your house if the husband dies. It's your most valuable asset.*" However, there are problems with this strategy. For example:

1. Mortgage protection coverage is essentially declining term insurance but often costs the same or even more than level term without the limited objective. Some "Mortgage Protection" policies are a little different from traditional because they are "first to die" policies—covering both spouses and pays when the first spouse dies. These products tend to be pricey compared to other term policies. Essentially, there is no advantage to buying a "specialty insurance" for which there is no specialty need.
2. Paying off the mortgage when an income earner dies can be helpful to the survivor by significantly reducing monthly expenses, but this payoff often isn't a necessity, and sometimes takes away from more important needs. More than likely, the mortgage wasn't going to be paid off in a lump sum on that particular date (date of death) but for the death of the insured. More to the point, the financial need of the survivor is not necessarily paying off the house. It's having enough money to pay the bills—all of them, not just the mortgage payment. There are times when having no mortgage payment offers substantial financial relief for the survivor, but insurance planning entails much more than simply buying a policy to fulfill one narrow purpose.

Level vs. Variable Premium—Level Term refers to a policy where the premium amount and the death benefit amount are precise and guaranteed without variation for the life of the contract.

By contrast, some term policies have scheduled premium increases. The idea is that the policy is more affordable in the early years when a person is starting out and cannot afford the full premium amount. Unfortunately, in most cases, being able to fully shop the market will yield level term policies that are not more expensive than those with rising premiums and the circumstance of payout always is the same (you die).

Permanent (Cash Value) Life Insurance is used when:

1. The death benefit is needed for an indefinite time.
2. The insurable term is for more than 30 years (maximum available in a Term Policy).

A cash value policy differs from a term policy in that the premium includes a third component: a cash accumulation account. The reason term insurance is inexpensive (and terminates) is that they terminate before the likelihood of death becomes high. Obviously, as people age, their likelihood of death increases, eventually rising to 100%. A life insurance policy that continues until death also has a 100% chance of paying out. Thus, the cost of insurance becomes very high. In the first several years of a cash value policy, the premium is more than the cost of insurance plus administrative expenses. This results in an accumulation of excess cash which then gets to grow through some formula. In later years when the cost of insurance rises and exceeds the premium, that cash value becomes the basis of paying the shortfall. Cash value policies are called "permanent" but that's not entirely true. Even "permanent" life insurance policies can have scheduled dates at which they lapse (end). However, the difference is that those theoretical lapse dates occur at ages well beyond an age at which anybody is reasonably expected to live. Therefore, while not technically permanent, they functionally are good until death.

There are two main types of permanent policies: Whole Life and Universal Life.

Whole Life (WL) offers fixed premiums and cash accumulation at a guaranteed rate. If the actual cash accumulation exceeds the guaranteed rate, then the excess is paid as a dividend which is often used to purchase additional coverage. These "paid up additions" can cause the death benefit to rise through time. However, in most cases, these increases are modest and most WL policies are scheduled to lapse between ages 95 and 100.

Universal Life (UL) offers flexibility in premiums as well as adjustable death benefit amounts. There are certain minimum guarantees, but the unguaranteed potential is much greater. Many UL policies have the capability to be guaranteed to much higher ages than WL, commonly to ages 120 or 121.

At one time, all permanent insurance was Whole Life. The concept of Universal Life was first proposed in the early 1970's and the first UL products were marketed in 1980. By 1985, UL sales exceeded WL and that trend continues today. The biggest reason for this is that UL policies offer much greater cash accumulation potential and therefore a greater amount of death benefit per premium dollar than WL. Thus, given identical premiums, the death benefit on a UL policy will usually be greater than a WL and even with paid-up additions, insureds seldom see the value of a WL policy exceed that of a UL.

Why is there still Whole Life?

One of the limitations of Universal Life is that policies must be relatively large. Only a handful of carriers offer coverage for less than $100,000 and none for less than $25,000. Whole Life policies, while potentially as large as an insurer is willing to permit, can also be written very small; as little as $5000. There are certainly situations where large Whole Life policies are desirable, but on the whole, the frequency of this is diminishing.

Final Expense Policy—Essentially this is a version of Whole Life insurance sufficient to pay for the cost of a funeral. These policies are typically written for amounts between $5000 and $50,000. Many commercial vendors—especially those mass-marketing products on TV, offer guaranteed issue "*You can't be turned down due to your health*." The reason for this is the insurance company covers their risk of paying too many claims too quickly by volume—and policy pricing. Essentially anything that is guaranteed issue is priced to include people who are way too unhealthy to get a policy that performs medical underwriting. In addition, the cost to an insurance company to check medical records on a $5000 insurance policy is greater than the money they'd make off the policy itself. However, someone in excellent health looking for a decent final expense policy would likely be better off applying for coverage that performs a full medical underwriting.

Kinds of Universal Life

Because Universal Life offers flexible premium, adjustable face and higher growth potential than Whole Life, many variants have developed to address different specific needs. Those differences primarily center on how the cash value account grows.

Straight Universal Life—These policies grow the cash value through fixed interest credits. Fundamentally those interest credits are linked to bond interest rates because the insurance company is required to maintain a minimum 100% reserve through top-rated bonds. Illustrations commonly show cash value accumulation tables for the guaranteed minimum interest rate and the "current" (but not guaranteed) interest rate and sometimes for an artificially determined "Midpoint" interest rate. Structuring a UL Policy based on the Guaranteed Rate is the safest but also the most expensive. Conversely structuring a plan on the "Current" rate is the most accurate and least expensive as long as interest rates do not fall below that of the "assumed rate." Sometimes, policies illustrated at the guaranteed rate and at the current rate are no different. Even more surprising is how much variation is possible in otherwise identical policies from different carriers. For example, it is possible that one carrier will have the lowest quote for a policy paid on one premium payment strategy but for not another. It is virtually impossible for a lay person to know how these subtle differences will play out and mass-marketing operations that tout "comparing companies" do not engage in that level of scrutiny. Relying on a professional, independent insurance advisor is the best way to accurately determine the best and most economical strategy.

Variable Universal Life (VUL)—A variable insurance product is a stock market investment. Unlike fixed insurance products that are regulated by a state's department of insurance, Variable insurance products are securities, regulated by FINRA (Financial **IN**dustry **R**egulatory **A**uthority). VULs rely on a portfolio of Mutual Funds as the basis of growing the cash value account. The advantage of this approach is much larger growth potential—provided markets continually rise. However, during times of market corrections (e.g., 2000-2002 and 2008), the loss of investment value also reduces the cash value in a VUL. However, the cost of insurance must still be paid from the account. If, between falling markets and withdrawals to pay future cost of insurance, the cash value reaches $0, there is a danger the policy can lapse (coverage terminates) and you're still alive.

Index Universal Life (IUL)—An outgrowth of the Index Annuity market, IUL policies offer cash value accumulation based on an indirect measure to a market index without exposure to the downsides of an actual market. Most IULs have both a minimum growth guarantee plus indexed growth opportunity allowing for much greater growth than Straight UL policies. Not only does the cash value in an IUL grow but so does the death benefit. While IULs may start out with less death benefit per premium dollar, in time the cash value growth and death benefit growth may substantially exceed that of a straight UL. However, death benefit growth does not occur immediately. Often it takes as much as 10 years before an IUL's death benefit starts to rise. Also, because death benefit increases are dependent on both account growth and cost of insurance, the younger a person is when purchasing an IUL, the better the overall result.

Survivor Universal Life (SUL) (AKA "Second-to-Die")—There are times, especially with regard to estate planning, that it is preferable to simultaneously insure both spouses and have the policy pay off at the *second* death. There are two advantages with this strategy:

1. The insurance companies regard simultaneously insuring two lives as less risky than insuring one. Thus, SULs are less expensive and may even insure a spouse who is otherwise not healthy enough to purchase an individual policy.
2. For estate planning purposes, the death benefit will be paid at the time that estate transfer must occur (the passing of the second spouse). Thus, from a timing perspective, it is far better suited than

making an "educated guess" as to which spouse will pass second or establishing a trust to "hold" the money if that "educated guess" is wrong.

Group Life (employers)—Employers commonly provide life insurance as an employee benefit. These policies are not written for the individual but rather for the company and extend to individual employees through a Certificate of Insurance. Coverage (and acceptance) is guaranteed but in most cases, when employment is terminated so is the coverage, or sometimes the death benefit is reduced. Group Life, especially when provided at no cost to the employee, is a valuable benefit (any benefit that's free is valuable). However, it should be regarded as supplemental; not your primary protection.

Reasons to have Life Insurance (Insurable Needs):

Financial Protection—Any time the death of a person would cause financial harm for someone else that is an ideal reason to have life insurance. The type and amount of insurance are directly dependent on the need but determining that need is more than simply picking some arbitrary amount that "sounds good." Under-insuring your actual need creates financial consequences later. Over-insuring your need costs more money—perhaps unnecessarily. Thus, insurance planning is a balancing act that is part of overall financial planning.

Business Planning—Life insurance serves a valuable function for business planning in several ways:

- **Key Man Insurance**—Many businesses rely heavily on certain individuals for the business' success. If that key person were to die, without being able to replace him/her effectively and quickly, the business could suffer, even irrevocably. Key Man Insurance is a policy owned by the company on the lives of one or more key personnel. In the event of their premature demise, the company collects a sum of money sufficient to recruit and hire a competent replacement.
- **Buy-Sell**—Many businesses are drawn up as partnerships between two or more individuals. If one of those partners should die, having a

life insurance policy permits the surviving partners to "buy out" the interest of that partner (from his/her estate). It is an effective way of not giving up important control of the company to parties who may not be skilled or interested in continuing the decedent's duties and yet not denying the decedent's fair share buy-out for that person's surviving family.

- **Non-Qualified Deferred Compensation Plans**—Large corporations commonly offer substantial financial incentives to high-level executives, including Non-Qualified Deferred Compensation Plans. These plans, primarily based on life insurance, are designed to grow cash value in the plan. At the executive's point of retirement, he/she can access the cash value in the plan as an income source, including receive the money in such a way that it is exempt from income tax. (More on this strategy later).

Estate Transfer Planning—Estate Planning is a complex area of planning that is best left to professionals to provide guidance. However, the following are a few basic considerations.

1. **Equitable Estate Settlement**—Often dividing even a simple estate can incur planning challenges. For example: A deceased couple had one house and two kids: Joe and Helen. Joe loves the house and wants to live in it forever. Helen hates it and wants to sell it as fast as possible. Neither has a lot of cash. A life insurance policy on the parents could provide Joe with enough liquidity to purchase Helen's interest in the house. This illustration is even more dramatic when considering the following actual case. A man, we'll call him Joe (not his actual name) owned an auto repair shop in the state where he and his wife raised their family. After retirement, Joe and his wife moved to southern state (to escape cold northern winters) but Joe's eldest son, who had long ago taken over the garage business stayed on to run it. It was his primary source of income. Joe also had two daughters, both living in the southern state (where they attended college and found husbands). Neither daughter had any interest in the auto shop nor in moving back up north but one of them lived

near-by and was interested in Joe's new house. The third daughter had no interest in that either. The garage was worth a lot of money; more than the house. Other than that, Joe had modest assets; clearly not enough to provide equal benefit to all three children when he and his wife were both gone. Therefore, Joe and his wife obtained a large Second-to-Die life insurance policy naming all three kids but providing different benefit amounts for each such that the total inheritance (including the garage, house, insurance policy plus all other assets) was equitable.

2. **Estate Tax Planning**—Large (multi-million dollar) estates are potentially subject to a wealth transfer tax called "Estate Tax" or "Inheritance Tax." Wealth Transfer Taxes occur when an estate is valued above a certain threshold. In 2017, that threshold for Federal tax was $5,490,000 (with some provisions that permit couples to combine individual exemptions). Some but not all states also impose a state estate or inheritance tax, but those that do, the exemption threshold is the same or less than the Federal exemption (cannot be more). Estates worth more than the threshold are taxed at 40% of the excess for Federal tax. That does not include any state inheritance tax. For example, assume the estate of a single person worth $6,490,000 died in 2017. That estate is worth $1,000,000 more than the $5,490,000 allowable exemption. The Federal Estate Tax will be $400,000, due within 9 months of the date of death.

There are a number of ways to address this liability but one of the simplest solutions is to purchase a life insurance policy large enough to cover the anticipated tax burden. However, simply buying a life insurance policy will not fix the problem and can even make it worse. How you own your life insurance policy can actually create additional tax liability.

Many advisors will tell you that life insurance proceeds are tax-free. What they really mean is that the death benefit is income tax free, although there are some exceptions to this. What is not said to you is that if you own your policy (the normal situation), your policy value is part of your estate for Estate Tax purposes and if you have a taxable estate, your policy will add a substantial tax burden to your estate. When Life insurance is considered an asset if owned by the deceased (or the deceased's estate), it is included in the estate for tax calculation purposes. In the above example, if the decedent had purchased a $1,000,000 life insurance policy, the estate is now $2,000,000 above the exemption and the tax due is $800,000; nearly the full value of the insurance policy.

Solution—However, if the policy is not owned by the decedent or his/her estate, in other words is owned "outside the estate," then the death benefit is not included as part of the estate's value and passes free of estate tax (plus income tax-free) to the beneficiaries. Simple? Well not entirely. There are two ways to establish a life insurance policy outside the estate:

A. Establish an irrevocable trust that owns the policy (commonly called "Irrevocable Life Insurance Trust" or "ILIT" for short). The policy is owned by the trust, and the trust is not part of the estate so neither is the insurance policy. The "trick" is in how the insurance policy, owned by the trust, gets its premiums paid.

The IRS holds that anything of value given by one person to another for less than a fair market value sale is a gift. This includes when insurance premiums are paid by one person (e.g., the insured) on a policy owned by someone else (the trust). IRS gift allowances (in 2017) are that any person may gift up to $14,000 to any other person (including the trust's named insurance beneficiaries) per year without having to file a gift tax return. A person who gifts more than $14,000 in one year to any one person, must file a Federal Gift Tax Return for the excess (IRS Form 709). The first $14,000 gifted is called the "Annual Gift Tax Exclusion" and does not require filing a Gift Tax return.

But, there is a "trap." The payment of an insurance premium by one person for the benefit of another is not a "present interest" gift; it is a "future interest gift." The IRS says that a future interest gift does not enjoy the annual exclusion. In other words, making premium payments into a life insurance policy is not an allowable gift because the recipient must wait until the future (when the donor dies) to receive the gift. Therefore, even though the trust was established "outside" the estate, making the premiums a future interest gift, causes a gift tax liability for the donor for every premium dollar paid, plus penalties and interest for failure to file a gift tax return. The tax, with the penalties and interest can exceed the death benefit of the policy. The key is not in the trust itself but rather how the premiums are paid. The secret is turning that potential "future interest" gift into a "present interest" gift that enjoys the $14,000 annual exclusion from Gift Tax and the eliminating the need to file a Gift Tax Return.

One "solution" arises from a 1968 court case (upholding a 1962 ruling of the Tax Court) called Crummey v. Commissioner. The outcome of this case was that in order for the gifted premium to be considered a present interest gift, the giftee (the insurance beneficiary) must be given the opportunity to take immediate possession of the gifted money. Therefore, when an ILIT is funded, every premium payment must be accompanied by a "Crummey Letter" which, in effect says to the insurance beneficiary "*You can immediately take the money that I have paid to the Trustee to pay for the life insurance policy. All you have to do is to tell the trustee that you want it. Let us know by X date. If not, it's going to pay for the insurance premium.*" Establishing and delivering Crummey Letters is not hard, but not knowing about it, or ignoring it to avoid the expense, can lead to costly mistakes. Record-keeping is also important including copies of every "Crummey Letter" should be retained and kept with the trust to be able to show to the IRS if asked. An Irrevocable Life Insurance Trust (ILIT) that is properly administered through until the life insurance is paid out is clearly the best methodology for owning a large life insurance policy.

B. An alternate strategy that avoids the need for a formal trust and

Crummey Letters is naming the beneficiaries as owners of the insurance policy. This effectively removes the policy from the insured's estate and provides an estate tax-free (and income tax-free) benefit. However, this strategy is not without its challenges or risks. First, because the beneficiaries now also own the policy, they could, if they wished, invade the policy's cash value, deplete it and cause the policy to lapse. Also, you can change the beneficiary designations at any time before your death; hence changes could be made that are not consistent with your intentions. This may not be a practical concern, but it's still important to know and consider these factors. Fortunately, there are ways to minimize the likelihood of it occurring if it is a concern. For example, if you make all your children co-owners of the policy, they would have to conspire together to change your intentions. If you have only one child, this strategy doesn't work.

Also, this strategy involves the same gifting issue as with the trust. The maximum allowable gift (of premiums) is (2017) $14,000 per donor per beneficiary per year. Also, if the premiums are paid directly into the policy without passing through the hands of the owner/beneficiary, it risks being regarded as a future gift and causing the insurance policy to be included in the estate. In other words, you can't pay the premium directly; you must gift the premium money to the policy owners (children) who then pay the premium for themselves. The simplest solution for this is to open a bank account in the name(s) of the owners/beneficiaries into which the premiums are gifted and from which the premiums are drafted.

C. Families that will never have Estate Tax or Inheritance Tax issues (because their estate value will not approach the exemption amount of $5.49 million in 2017) can simply own their life insurance policy and pay for the premiums themselves. They should know that the policy value will be included in their estate for Estate Tax purposes if their estate value should rise to the exemption amount, or if the exemption amount should be reduced. The only problem with this strategy is that tax policy changes frequently, and even though there is no problem based upon current law, the laws will change over time. Hence you must not assume that future changes in the law will be favorable to you.

With good financial and estate planning, these challenges are minor technicalities that are easily overcome. Your unintended mistakes are very costly to those you leave behind. Knowing what must be done and how to do it is critical.

Using Life Insurance before dying

Many cash value life insurance policies permit the owner's access to both death benefit and cash value accounts without having to die.

Accelerated Death Benefit Rider—Some cash value policies include a built-in feature that permits access to the face (or death benefit) amount for medical need. Generally, these provisions permit a person to receive death benefit proceeds if diagnosed with certain critical or chronic illnesses, require hospice care or are confined in a Long-Term Care facility. Details vary but generally the provision is that upon diagnosis and certification by a physician, a stated percentage (e.g., 2% per month) of the face amount is payable directly to the insured. For example, a $250,000 policy with a 2% accelerated benefit rider would pay $5000/month for these needs, including Long Term Care. Because payments come from the death benefit, they are not taxable as income. The payments simply reduce the death benefit dollar-for-dollar.

Accessing Cash Value—Permanent policies that build cash value permit access to that cash value in two ways: as a direct cash withdrawal and as a loan. When cash value is withdrawn the portion that was equivalent to premium paid is not taxable but excess (through growth) is taxed at ordinary income tax rates (not as long term capital gain). Conversely, taking a loan against the policy is not a taxable event and if the loan is never repaid (you're borrowing the money from yourself) the loan amount, as a percentage of the total cash value, reduces the death benefit amount proportionally.

Prior to 1988, it was common place for wealthy people to purchase large life insurance policies, overfund them and later withdraw the accumulated cash value (which had grown considerably) as a policy loan that was never to be repaid (not caring if the death benefit remained or not). Then in October 1988, Congress passed the Technical and Miscellaneous Revenue Act. TAMRA specified that when a life insurance policy is funded faster than a designated rate (called the "Seven-Pay Guidelines Test") the policy becomes a "Modified Endowment Contract" or "MEC." When withdrawing cash value from a MEC, including policy loans, the withdrawals are regarded as coming out LIFO (Last In First Out) meaning taxable until only principal (premiums paid) remain. In addition, withdrawing cash value in a MEC by an owner younger than 59½, could also incur a 10% tax penalty.

When an insurance policy is <u>not</u> a MEC (meets the Seven Pay Guidelines Test), direct withdrawals of cash value are FIFO (First In, First Out) and withdrawals by loan are tax exempt. Obviously, any policy intended for cash value access should be a Non-MEC insurance policy.

Retirement Income Planning—One of the greatest uses of cash value insurance, when a Non-MEC, is to grow the cash value for an extended time and then use it (as a Policy Loan) for future income. This strategy, very similar to the corporate Non-Qualified Deferred Compensation Plans, is available to anyone who is insurable and has a long enough time horizon for the growth to be useful. In particular, this strategy is where IULs are the most attractive.

For example, a parent purchases a policy on their young child and funds it until that child is through college, after which the insurance policy simply sits and grows. When that child reaches retirement age, the cash value in that policy may have grown to $1 Million or more and he/she may access the cash value as a tax-free loan to generate income. When established correctly, relatively nominal premium payments could provide a six-figure, tax-free retirement income for life—and still reserve a death benefit to protect his/her future family when he/she dies.

The dilemma for future generations is that life expectancies are increasing while retirement saving is becoming more difficult. The elimination of pensions, declining value of Social Security, reduced salaries and benefits paid by companies with no loyalty to its employees are all trends that do not bode well. Therefore, this strategy is something every well-to-do family should seriously consider for their children and grandchildren.

Tax implications of life insurance

In most cases, the death benefit proceeds from life insurance are not taxable as income. This is what everyone expects, but there are exceptions to the general rule that death benefit proceeds are tax-free. The three most common exceptions are:

1. **Transfer for value**—If the ownership of a life insurance policy is transferred to another owner where consideration is exchanged, then the proceeds paid to the beneficiary becomes taxable income. This happens frequently with policies that are owned by businesses. It can also happen with policy transfers relating to government assistance planning or other reasons. This same bad result occurs when ownership is transferred and there is a loan outstanding on the policy. That circumstance creates a transfer for value resulting in the death benefit being taxable income. Hence, anytime the ownership of a life insurance policy is being transferred for any reason, be cautious and seek professional counsel to make sure it is accomplished without creating a tax liability.
2. **Interest on payouts** – When beneficiaries elect to receive a death benefit as income rather than lump sum, any interest earned on that benefit amount will be taxable as income. However, payout installments are made on an "Exclusion Ratio" basis meaning a portion of each payment consists of principal and a portion is the interest. Only the interest portion is taxable.
3. **Profit from life insurance settlements** – A Life Insurance Settlement is an arrangement where a policy is sold to another party. The policy

remains in force. The buyer assumes the premiums and receives the death benefit. But, the amount of settlement may be taxable if it exceeds the amount of premium paid in prior to the settlement sale. However, as an exception to the exception, under the Pension Protection Act, if the proceeds are paid to you as long term care payments (reimbursements for medical/long term care expenses), then the money is treated as a tax-free exchange. Proceeds exceeding those expenses would be taxed to you as ordinary income.

Upgrading Insurance Policies

Many people with existing cash value insurance plans can make them bigger and better at no cost. Life expectancies are continually increasing but insurance companies infrequently update the mortality tables they use. Policies are priced from mortality tables used at the time of policy creation and once a policy is issued, there is no credit for increasing longevity. The conclusion is that many older life insurance policies are "over-priced." If you are still in good health, the solution is to "swap" your current policy for one that offers more death benefit or the same death benefit at lower premium. There is no cost to these swaps (called 1035 or tax-free exchanges). Often a 1035 exchange can result in very substantial premium savings or improvements to your policy, including higher death benefit or included an accelerated death benefit rider.

The success of these swaps is entirely dependent on underwriting (based upon your current health) but having a consultation with an independent insurance professional (with access to the widest possible array of carriers) is a very effective, no risk way to find out. Also, under the Pension Protection Act, 1035 exchanges have been expanded to allow life insurance policies and annuities to be swapped for policies with long term care benefits with no taxable event.

MONEY SECRET: Life Insurance Planning is one of the most important areas of planning that everyone should do. It is not just about protecting a loved one from your premature death, but also can be the centerpiece of sound retirement planning, estate planning, tax planning, medical care planning and so forth. The bottom line is that life insurance can be asset protected and tax sheltered. Because the breadth of possibilities are vast and so much of the devil being in the details, Life Insurance planning should only be done in direct consultation with an insurance planning professional and should not be sought through online offerings or because a mass-marketing company has operators conveniently standing by to take your order.

CHAPTER 8
ANNUITY MYTH-BUSTING

A mere mention of the word "Annuity" will elicit all sorts of reactions, many visceral both for and against. But a knee-jerk response to a word does not help in your understanding these insurance contracts. Annuities come in many shapes and colors. One may be perfect for your situation while another can be detrimental. Your understanding of the key elements of any proposal is essential. Getting good professional advice from an independent advisor who deals in many financial strategies (not merely sells annuities) may be your best way to determine if an annuity is right for your unique situation and if so, which one.

What is an Annuity? An annuity is nothing more, or less, than an account with an insurance company. Traditionally, the term dates back to the days of the Roman Empire when people would make a single large payment into a contract called "annua" (from the Latin meaning "annual payments") that converted that sum into income the person could not outlive. Roman soldiers, for example, were provided annuity compensation for their military service.

During the Middle Ages, annuities were used by kings and feudal lords as payments to investors who financially supported the cost of waging wars. In 1720, the Presbyterian Church introduced annuities into the American colonies to provide a secure retirement to aging clergy and their families, later expanding that service to orphans and widows. Benjamin Franklin bequeathed annuities to the cities of Philadelphia and Boston. Boston's paid out through the 1990s until the city elected to receive the balance in lump sum. Babe Ruth invested 100% of his net worth in annuities and avoided losses during the great depression. He famously said: "*I may take risks in life, but I will never risk my money, I use annuities and I never have to worry about my money.*"

Today, the largest annuity in the United States is Social Security; the second largest include corporate pensions. In both cases, an established sum of money is converted into a lifetime income payment.

Much of the bad press surrounding annuities—and there's a lot of it—stems from misinformation, often perpetuated by people in the financial services world who cannot sell them.

Common annuity myths:

Annuities are too complex for the average person to understand.

There are literally thousands of different annuity products in existence and they can be vastly different. Some are extremely simple. Others are more sophisticated and many do vastly different things. Trying to understand all annuities as though they were one creates an artificial appearance of complexity that is neither accurate nor realistic.

Annuities lock your money up and you can never get at it.

While annuities are time deposits, they all offer some level of short-term liquidity and most permit complete, penalty-free access for certain emergencies. Further, some annuities have longer commitment terms than others. Purchasing an annuity with an unsuitably long time horizon was not the fault of the industry. It was the fault of an over-eager sales person or lack of basic scrutiny by the purchaser.

If you die, the insurance company keeps your money.

In a word: nonsense. The only time when something along

these lines can occur is when you annuitize the contract (meaning exchange the account value for a lifetime of income), then die. But there are scores of different ways to receive money—even lifetime income from an annuity without electing a life-only payment schedule. And it's a personal choice to elect a single life-only payment schedule. Nobody is required to use that strategy.

Annuities all have huge fees.

Some annuities (mostly Variable Annuities) carry fees and at times they can add up. However, there are plenty of annuities with small and even no fees and in some cases, annuity products with no fees of any kind can offer respectable returns including returns on par with other non-annuity investments.

TYPES OF ANNUITIES

There are two broad categories of annuities: Fixed and Variable and those are unfortunate terms because they don't actually mean what people typically think they mean. Commonly taken to mean how growth is credited, with annuities the terms "Fixed" and "Variable" refer to how the money is held, not how it grows.

FIXED ANNUITY—This is a pure insurance product. Technically, an annuity is "Fixed" when the deposited money—called a premium—plus all credited growth, may be comingled with the general funds account of the insurance company. This means the insurance company has access to the money to make money for itself.

Many people believe that insurance companies invest those deposits, whether in the stock market, or by purchasing real estate, etc. but that's not true. By law, insurance companies *must* secure the deposits (and the credited gains) with a minimum 100% reserves and that means bonds. But insurance companies are not permitted to just go out and buy anybody's bond. Those bonds not only must be investment grade (highly rated) they must be approved by the NAIC (National Association of Insurance Commissioners) which is a collective organization of all 56 states departments of insurance (50 regular states, DC and 5 offshore US Territories). The insurance companies then take the coupon (interest) payments earned, and from that, pay themselves and their employees, pay the agent, etc. and then are free to invest the remainder in ways they elect (subject to permissibility and regulatory oversight by the NAIC). Thus, the term "Fixed" technically means this direct comingling of funds. Functionally it also means the annuity purchaser is free from risk associated with falling markets because fixed annuities are not investments and cannot be exposed to investment risk whatsoever. Finally, because fixed annuities offer the insurance company potential profits by holding the money, they do not charge large asset management fees.

Within the scope of Fixed Annuities, there are three distinct subgroups, each with specific benefits and trade-offs:

a. **Fixed Immediate Annuity** or SPIA ("Single Premium Immediate Annuity"). These products instantly convert a sum of money into a finite income stream. That income may be scheduled to last for a stated number of years guaranteed, for a person's entire lifetime, for the lives of two people (usually spouses) or a suite of different combinations.

b. **Multi-year Fixed Deferred Annuity** or MYGA ("Multi-Year Guaranteed Annuity). These are CD-like Annuities in that the annuity guarantees a stated amount of interest for a specified period of time. After that term, the annuity owner may withdraw the annuity or continue it at a rate to be determined by the company.

c. **Fixed Index Annuity** or FIA (formerly called "Equity Index Annuity"). First launched in 1995, Index Annuities offer growth by *indirect* relation to a stock market index. The annuity owner is not invested in the stock market in any capacity, not exposed to market risk and does not pay asset management fees (there's nothing to manage). Rather, the insurance company applies interest (called "Index Credits") to the account based on a formula which measures a market index. If the index posts a gain, that gain is posted to the account. If the index posts a loss, there is no harm because losses are not deducted.

The array of index annuity products is vast, but many impose secondary growth limiters which can result in enormous differences in result. Especially since the end of the mortgage crisis of 2008, the majority of these limiters comes in the form of growth caps. A cap is essentially a ceiling on the maximum amount of growth that will be credited regardless of how good the index performed. For example, if a market index posts a real return of 18%, an index annuity with a 3.5% cap will credit only 3.5%. Conversely, if next year, the index then falls 20%, the annuity receives a 0% for no loss.

A few Index Annuities offer uncapped growth meaning, in this simplified example, the owner would receive 18% interest in the first year and 0% the second. There are hundreds of Index Annuity products in existence and some are clearly better than others. The best way to find an ideal Index Annuity is to work with an unbiased, independent professional who can legitimately shop the marketplace, and ignore all the anti-annuity internet hype.

Clearly, an appropriate Fixed Index Annuity offers retirees and other risk adverse investors a potential opportunity to capture market-level gains without the downside risk of market loss. There may be other factors that should be considered, but if market risk is the thing that causes loss of sleep, stress, etc. a good Fixed Index Annuity, especially one without a growth cap may be the best way to protect your nest-egg without sacrificing growth potential.

VARIABLE ANNUITY—This is a security (stock market) investment, sold exclusively by securities-licensed people, primarily through a Broker-Dealer. In a Variable Annuity, the deposited funds plus any growth credited must be held in a separate account. In other words, the insurance company has no direct access to, nor any ability to make money from the money. Accordingly, they must impose a fee structure to pay for operations and remain profitable.

Fees—Some annuity nay-sayers proclaim that "annuities have high and hidden fees" as justification to avoid them. To begin with, state insurance law requires that all fees be disclosed in writing, not hidden in fine print or buried deep within the contract. However, most financial accounts, even banking, have fees of some sort. All financial advisors charge fees or commissions or both; many charge a percentage of your account, whether money is made or lost. The mere existence of a fee means nothing. What's relevant is the size of the fee in relation to the benefit it offers. When the benefit being received in exchange for the fee is appropriate and reasonable, so is the fee. When not, then not.

To be fair, some fixed annuities also have fees, generally in exchange for specific benefits called riders. But in most cases, those riders are optional. Finally, if avoiding a fee is your only consideration, nothing that is stock market-based will be for you and there are plenty of banking and fixed annuities that charge no fees of any kind.

Access to Money—Sometimes people accuse that annuities "lock your money up" and prevent access to it. Annuities are time deposits—meaning they are not to be used as a short-term growth vehicle but to be fair bonds and CDs are also time deposits. In a bond, an investor commits to a term as long as 30 years (there are no 30-year annuities). The bond pays a fixed income (called a coupon) after which, at maturity, the bond repays the principal. If a bond is sold early, and if interest rates have risen since the purchase of the bond, the investor may lose principal. Typical CDs are also time deposits which commonly impose a penalty on any premature withdrawal. Conversely, annuities permit partial access to the money without penalty. The amount is dependent on the actual contract but commonly is around 10% of the account value. As such, they can be more liquid than a bond or CD. Furthermore, the penalty amount declines annually until you have penalty-free access to your entire account. The penalty period varies with each product and should be considered against the benefits the product offers. The process of selecting an annuity product should include relative liquidity including the length of the penalty period.

Finally, most insurance companies have strict financial underwriting guidelines. If an agent submits an annuity application that ties up too much of a client's money in that annuity, the issuing company will reject the application.

Most annuities permit access in several different ways.

1. **Lump Sum**—At the end of the required deferral period, an annuity may be partially or completely liquidated without penalty. Most annuities do not require liquidation at the end of this period, only that a penalty for doing so has disappeared.
2. **Discretionary Access**—Most annuities permit penalty-free access even during this initial required deferral period, commonly around 10% per year. Access can be by lump sum withdrawal or as an income (monthly, quarterly, etc.). An annuity owner who desires money need only contact the carrier. If no money is desired then that decision is entirely at the discretion of the owner.
3. **Required Minimum Distributions**—Annuities can be IRAs, just like any other sort of financial account. When an annuity is also an IRA and the owner is 70½ or older, the annuity will automatically calculate and pay the Required Minimum Distribution penalty-free, regardless of the "usual" rules of discretionary access.
4. **Income**—Annuities can generate income in four ways:
    a. **Income through discretionary withdrawals**. An annuity owner may elect to receive a monthly income from the annuity simply by exercising the penalty-free withdrawal privilege. Other than reducing (by withdrawal) the account's value, this manipulation has no effect on the annuity's growth rate.
    b. **Required Minimum Distributions—**These mandatory withdrawals are income. Sometimes people find that supplementing their retirement income with a lifetime of Required Minimum Distributions, provides the added financial cushion they need to supplement their Social Security and pensions to enjoy their retirement years. As one gets older, the Required Minimum Distribution increases each year as a percentage of the account. In most cases, the Required Minimum Distribution does reduce how much discretionary money may also be withdrawn during the penalty period.

c. **Traditional Annuitization**—As with a traditional corporate pension, this is a conversion of a defined sum of money into a series of payments for one or two lives, or for a specified number of years or a combination of both. With rare exception, there is little or no growth offered once the payments begin and the income election is permanent. Some people criticize that this manipulation effectively removes any growth credited or that "*If you die, the insurance company keeps your money*." However, the only time this becomes an issue is when a person elects single life annuitization with no other provisions to return the principal. There are times when such a strategy is legitimate but it is a relatively rare income election choice and when a mistake is made, more often than not, it is the fault of the sales agent, not the annuity product itself. Life-only payouts provide more income than the other strategies. Therefore, this election may be appropriate for someone who needs maximum guaranteed lifetime income without regard to heirs, especially if they expect to live a long time.

d. **Income Riders**—These features allow a contract to be converted into a lifetime income that does not exchange the base account for the income and can even permit the base account to grow, leaving the undistributed amount to remain as a death benefit. If a person lives a very long time, their income payments may exceed the entire contract's account value (plus growth). In this case, there is no residual death benefit. However when the annuity owner dies with cash still in the account, this becomes a death benefit payable to the beneficiaries. In addition, some products permit the income to be turned off and turned back on again as future needs change. Some income riders charge a fee. Others do not, although those that do tend to offer more income and better benefits than those that don't. Generally, the amount of income generated by an income rider is less (per dollar of account value) than by traditional annuitization but when added to the death benefit, income riders are often more attractive.

In addition, many income rider products use accelerated growth formulae to generate the income account, so that the end result is that the net income may be greater. For example: Suppose a traditional annuity grows $100,000 to $120,000 before lifetime payout begins. Assume the annuitant's life expectancy is 20 years. His life payout will be $500/month ($120,000 divided over 20 years or $6000/year). In other words, the annuity factor is 5% (5% X $120,000 = $6000). Conversely, suppose an annuity with an income rider pays out at 4.5%. However, because of enhanced growth, the annuity has grown from $100,000 to $150,000 over the same time frame. The 4.5% payout factor now provides a lifetime income of $6750/year ($562.50/month).

Some ideal uses of annuities—Before talking about whether annuities are good or bad, it's important to note that no annuity is right for everybody nor is any annuity right for anybody's every dollar. Annuities serve a valuable purpose when used correctly and in conjunction with carefully thought-out objectives. The following represents a partial list of common uses for each main product category. This list is by no means exhaustive or absolute.

Variable Annuity—One of the best uses of a Variable Annuity is by a self-employed person seeking to build his/her own retirement account. Most Variable Annuities permit unlimited deposits, occasionally with matching contributions by the issuing company. Because annuities grow tax-deferred, the annuity owner has a place to make regular contributions, benefit from the ability to move from investment to investment without incurring capital gains tax on the trade, receive the benefits of dollar cost averaging (a process which makes regular investing during volatile markets more attractive than a buy and hold strategy) and of course, the advantage of "triple compounding" (growth on principal plus growth on growth plus growth on tax-deferred amount). If the Variable Annuity selected also offers deposit bonuses, then each deposit receives the equivalent of "matching money" from the annuity company.

Immediate and Deferred Fixed Annuities—There are times when guarantees are more important than growth opportunity. This is particularly true when a person's time horizons for retirement (or other income need) are precise and known. In addition, sometimes a person needs a fixed payment schedule to obtain something else, for example, a large life insurance policy. Using an immediate annuity to purchase the insurance policy guarantees the premium payments will continue for life (after which time, the insurance pays out and needs no further premium). This strategy may be very helpful for someone whose income varies from year to year or who has a significant financial obligation that will continue past retirement.

Fixed Index Annuity—These are ideally suited for people who seek safety with growth potential, especially with money they are very unlikely to liquidate in lump sum. Foremost would include an IRA or 401(k), etc. As already noted, with these products the devil is in the details but as a general guideline, products that are uncapped offer better upside results than those with growth caps. Again, ask an unbiased, independent professional for recommendations.

MONEY SECRET: Annuities offer potential benefits that are not available with other types of financial products. This makes them potentially attractive as part of a bigger financial picture. No product, not even the best annuity product, can satisfy everyone's financial needs. Only someone with a state insurance license can sell an annuity and only someone who also has a securities license can sell a Variable Annuity. Avoid advice from anyone who is not properly licensed and only seek advice from licensed professionals who are truly independent (not employed by a commercial financial entity). Further, it often helps to seek advice from a professional who can offer optional investments other than annuities, but look critically at the pros and cons of any investment. As with other things in life, if you seek a solution from a carpenter with only a hammer and nail, the solution offered will be the nail. The bottom line is that many people will find that an annuity can be an appropriate and safe investment to diversify their overall investment plan.

CHAPTER 9
TRUST BASED PLANNING

Everyone needs a plan for transferring assets after their death. Fundamentally, there are three basic types:

1. **No Formal Plan**—More correctly known as "Intestacy" or dying without a valid Will or other formal statement of desires. For anyone with no formal plan, the states have a default plan to handle the distribution of the decedent's assets. Intestacy rules vary from state to state but regardless of state, your heirs will not likely be happy with the outcome because rarely does the state distribute your assets the way you would choose. Having no plan is not planning.
2. **Will-based Planning**—A Will is a formal statement of your wishes and desired for asset transfer. However, a Will is *not* an outright binding declaration of what must happen. Rather it's your request to the Probate Court that, provided there are no conflicting issues, will (eventually) be honored. But far too often, things are not as simple as people believe.

   First of all, a Will does <u>not</u> avoid probate; it requires probate. In fact, the technical definition of "Probate" is "Proving the Will." The Probate Court's job is to determine if the paper presented to the court is actually your Last Will and Testament and if contested, that you were competent and not unduly influenced when you signed that paper. Also, the court determines that your named assets were, in fact, owned by you and owned outright—and just because you say so, doesn't make it true. More to the point, since you're dead, the court has no way to know one way or the other. Some of the potential issues may include if there are any liens or other creditors or unnamed heirs with a legitimate interest or potential ownership share in the estate. The court may need to verify who the beneficiaries really are, giving fair opportunity for any unnamed beneficiary to step forward and present a claim. Probate can be a time-consuming and expensive process and any cost associated with Probate is paid out of the estate first. Of course, this may mean that an asset designated for inheritance is now no longer available.

There are times when good Will-based planning is entirely appropriate. Especially when estates are simple and assets modest, a good Will may be completely adequate.

However, one common mistake with Will based planning is to think that your Will controls how all your property is distributed at your death. For most married couples and many others, your Last Will and Testament controls very little. Things you say in your Will may be superseded by how you own title to your property. For example, married couples commonly own their real estate as Tenants by the Entireties or as Joint with Rights of Survivorship. This means the surviving Tenant (joint owner) gets that real estate regardless of what the Will says. Similar, many people have their bank and investment accounts held jointly with rights of survivorship. This gives the same result. Life insurance, annuity contracts, and retirement accounts are all distributed by Beneficiary Designation; not by your Will. Sometimes people sign a contract at the bank or with their investment broker to distribute their account by "Pay on Death" (POD) or "Transfer on Death" (TOD). These documents give the account a beneficiary designation which bypasses the Will.

3. **Trust-based Planning**—Essentially a Trust is a contract for which there are three parties:

- Grantor—The creator of the trust (also called Trustor, Settlor, Trust-maker)
- Trustee—The manager of trust who is appointed by the Grantor
- Beneficiary—Anybody the trust was created to benefit, including the Grantor.

Trusts can be used by anyone and can accomplish a wide variety of planning goals and they fall into two broad categories Revocable and Irrevocable

Revocable Trusts, especially Revocable Living Trusts are commonly used to avoid probate. More importantly, they allow the Grantor to leave their property to whom they want, when they want, how they want, and all at the lowest possible cost. In most cases, the Grantor of a Revocable Trust is also the Trustee and the Beneficiary. Upon the Grantor's death, a successor Trustee, named in the trust is designated to assume control of the trust along with specific instructions, naming the successor beneficiaries and under what circumstances may they receive assets from the Trust.

Because the Grantor is also Trustee and Beneficiary (meaning the Trustee has full, unfettered access to everything the trust owns), the IRS is entirely uninterested in regulating or overseeing revocable trusts. They require no separate tax ID number and no separate income tax filing. They're considered a "pass through" entity and are treated the same as the Grantor, using the Grantor's Social Security number as the trust's tax identification number. Thus, a Revocable Trust is not an entity separate from the individual. However, for a trust to work as intended, the property must be transferred to the trustee—meaning ownership (title) of the property must be transferred from the name of the Grantor to the Trustee to be administered pursuant to the trust agreement. Fundamentally, a Trust that owns nothing controls nothing and it's little more than a stack of paper with writing on it.

While a Revocable Trust can do a lot more than bypass Probate, one of the things it cannot do is protect assets from creditors of the Grantor (while the Grantor is living). Because the Trust and Grantor are the same, anything the Trust owns is subject to the same liabilities as the Grantor. However, Trust-based planning offers many benefits to the family when the Grantor dies:

- Assets are handled privately, not through court system
- The transfers usually proceed much more quickly
- Trust can be set up to handle inequitable distribution of assets, protect beneficiaries from secondary claims a spouse's remarriage, protect the children from a divorce or in-laws of the beneficiaries, and the ability to provide for different personalities in same family: one a spender, another a saver, etc.
- Trusts can be used for income tax planning, estate tax planning, and generation skipping tax planning.

The initial cost of establishing a trust is more than the cost of a Will, but at the death of a Grantor, a trust commonly saves a significant sum compared to Will based planning. Normally, the cost of court (Probate Court costs money), plus higher professional fees (lawyer, CPA, etc.) for transferring assets through Probate, add up to far more than the cost of avoiding it by use of a trust.

Irrevocable Trusts are different in that the Beneficiary is not the Grantor and in most cases, the Grantor is not the Trustee. In other words, once an Irrevocable Trust is established, the Grantor no longer has personal access to the money or the assets held in the trust. Irrevocable Trusts generally (but not always) take the asset out of the Grantor's estate, thereby eliminating its exposure to Estate or Inheritance Tax. However, an Irrevocable Trust reduces or eliminates the Grantor's control over trust assets in direct contrast to a revocable trust.

There are a number of different types of Irrevocable Trusts—far too many to cover here in detail. Each accomplishes a different planning objective. Some of the more common types are:

Irrevocable Life Insurance Trust (ILIT)—These were discussed in Chapter 7 (Life Insurance Planning). Essentially the trust owns the life insurance policy so the death benefit goes to beneficiaries without adding to an Estate Tax liability.

Charitable Trusts—Like the ILIT, Charitable Trusts bequeath large sums of money to charitable entities. In setting them up, the Grantor not only gets to avoid taxes (income and inheritance tax), the Grantor may be able to receive a tax deduction based on the value of the donated assets. However, the IRS is not blind. Claiming a charitable deduction solely to get the deduction (with no genuine interest in the charity being supported) may cause the IRS to invalidate the tax advantage as a sham. In other words, the primary purpose of establishing the Charitable Trust *must* be to benefit the charity. There are many variations of Charitable Trusts, the most common two being:

- **Charitable Remainder Trust**—is where the charity gets the trust's accounts when the Grantor dies and while alive, the Grantor gets the income from whatever the Trust earns or as a percentage of assets. These trusts can be set up for the income to continue for one or more than one lives. The charitable deduction is based upon the life expectancies of the income beneficiaries.
- **Charitable Lead Trust**—is where the charity gets the income generated through the Grantor's death (or earlier if so specified), and then other beneficiaries get the trust accounts. Normally it takes about a 20 year term for the Grantor's estate to avoid estate tax related to the assets used to create the trust.

Credit Shelter and Generation-Skipping Trusts—are designed to move assets (other than life insurance) to heirs without incurring estate taxes through two generations. These irrevocable trusts are frequently used in Revocable Living Trusts and are created at the death of the Grantor.

Qualified Terminal Interest Property (QTIP) Trust—is a Trust that allows the Grantor to provide for a surviving spouse while also maintaining control of how the trust's assets are distributed once the surviving spouse dies. This type of irrevocable trust is frequently used within a Revocable Living Trusts and is created at the death of the Grantor.

Qualified Personal Residence Trust (QPRT)—is a Trust that shelters a home from estate and inheritance taxes by taking the home out of the Grantor's estate. These trusts are time sensitive in that you *cannot* set them up just before death. Then normally the Grantor must pay rent to the Trustee.

Supplemental and Special Needs Trusts—are not for estate tax avoidance purposes but rather to control access to, use by, and distribution of assets for the benefit of others after the Grantor has passed. Supplemental Needs Trusts are often created in one's Will for the benefit of one's surviving spouse, particularly when the spouse is sick or frail. Special Needs Trusts normally are created as separate trusts for the benefit of a "special need's" child or children. Supplemental and Special Needs Trusts specifically are designed to allow the beneficiary to become eligible for or to remain on Medicaid or other government assistance for their lifetime. These trusts can be difficult to manage and often require professional administration. There are several technical variations on these trusts but essentially, they all serve the same broad purpose.

MONEY SECRET: Trust planning is a very powerful tool for good estate planning. Trusts can accomplish a lot of things that nothing else can achieve including saving thousands of dollars in fees, taxes, and costs, saving time and headaches in Probate Court, allowing you to control distribution of assets for the benefit and protection of beneficiaries and to create distinct tax advantages. However, Trust planning is sometimes complex and selecting the right kind of trust is only half the battle. A well drafted Trust is far superior to one that is not. Many general practice lawyers dabble in trust planning but just because it's called "The Practice of Law" doesn't mean you want them practicing on you. Something you find on-line is even worse. The sad truth is that a layman cannot tell the difference between a good trust document and a poorly drafted trust document by reading it. Only an attorney who specializes in Trust Planning can offer the most effective and robust Trust documents with professional guidance to meet your planning goals.

CHAPTER 10
TAX PLANNING IS FINANCIAL PLANNING

There is a significant difference between a Tax Preparer and a Tax Planner. A Tax Preparer calculates how much tax is due based on what you earned last year and prepares the documentation required to report it. A Tax Planner adds to that, strategies to use going forward to reduce and improve next year's tax exposure.

Before exploring some basic ideas about tax planning, it's important to understand how income tax is calculated. Fundamentally, an income tax return (Form 1040) has two sides. On the front, you add and subtract all the reportable items that lead to an amount to be entered on Line 37 at the bottom of the page called the Adjusted Gross Income (AGI). This is literally (and figuratively) the "Bottom Line" and is the amount of income that is taxable. But taxable is not necessarily taxed. After calculating AGI, you turn the form over and complete the second side. Here, deductions and other reductions are subtracted from your AGI to determine the total amount of income that you actually owe. Side one of Form 1040 determines your *taxable* income. Side two determines how much your income is actually *taxed*.

Income Tax reduction strategies then proceed from two platforms:

1. How can you reduce your AGI (without reducing your actual or gross income)?
2. How can you increase your deductions to lessen how much of the AGI is actually taxed?

Good Tax Planning starts with the previous year; a straight income tax return. But then it continues to explore ways to improve these two basic areas: reduce AGI, increase deductions.

Most people are familiar with the concept of increasing deductions as a tax reduction strategy. Fewer appreciate the importance of AGI reduction. However, dollar-for-dollar, reducing AGI has a greater impact on total tax reduction because by reducing AGI, some deductions are simultaneously increased.

One of the problems that plague many tax filers, especially small business owners, is filing late—even if legally with an extension. The reason is that by the time the return is complete, half or more of the year may be gone. Preparing last year's return cannot fix this year, but waiting half a year to discover fixable mistakes may make fixing those mistakes difficult until next year.

Also, always looking at taxes only one year at a time fails to take in the big picture. Good tax planning should project outward 3-5 years and even more although tax laws do constantly change.

Tax law changes occur in two variations:

Minor adjustments—that may require slight to actual tax preparation but do not significantly alter the big picture.

Major changes—that require wholesale planning changes.

Every change to the tax code is beneficial to some and detrimental to others. The key is in knowing what the changes are and seeking lawful ways to reduce your tax load, if possible.

Pay tax on what you receive, not what you don't

One of the more common tax planning mistakes that people make is generating income that is taxed but not received or needed. There are several sources where people commonly generate taxable events on money they never receive and may never get to spend.

Dividend Payments on non-qualified investments generate a taxable event whether the dividend payment is taken or not. While there are certainly advantages to investment dividends, the tax liability is not to be ignored. Worse is that dividends are taxed as ordinary income whether received or reinvested. Conversely, growth (capital appreciation) is taxed only upon receipt and generally at a lesser rate (long-term capital gain). With dividend payments, the double whammy is that if after the dividend is generated, the investment loses value (market loss) you are still liable for tax on money that no longer exists.

Portfolio Turnover—occurs when investment positions are bought and sold, whether by fund managers trading stocks or by you, the gains are reported as income. Where those gains occurred over more than one calendar year, they are taxed at the lower long-term capital gain rate. When those gains occur within the same calendar year, they are taxed at the higher short-term rate; the same rate as ordinary income. While there are justifiable reasons for portfolios to be rebalanced, doing so too frequently can generate taxable consequences that are greater than the benefit from having made the trade.

Certificates of Deposit (CDs)—(and other simple interest-bearing instruments) report the interest credits as taxable income even though you never actually received the money. In fact, CDs typically do not permit penalty-free access to the money until maturity which means you paid tax on income you did not, and could not, without a penalty, receive. Obviously with current interest rates being as low as they are, this is a minor concern. However, prior to the housing crisis or 2007, CDs paid 4-6% interest and much more than that in years past.

Bonds—pay a coupon (interest), usually every 6 months. Except for tax-free (municipal) bonds, those income payments are reported as ordinary taxable income. But when it comes to calculating tax on Social Security, even those tax-free payments from municipal bonds count toward determining how much Social Security gets taxed. Thus, while the muni bond income itself is not taxed, that income can generate a taxable event by triggering or increasing income tax on your Social Security payments. In addition, the income also can significantly increase your Medicare premiums which are adjusted annually based upon your previous year's income tax return.

Employer-based Qualified Retirement Plans:

Defined Contribution Plans such as a 401(k), 403(b), 457, etc. enjoy the benefit of the contributions being invested on a pre-tax basis, meaning the money is deferred from tax. Many times, employers provide matching money based on employee contributions, to a stated limit. Employees should always take advantage of Employer matching promises. Sometimes this is described as "Free Money" but it's not. It's actually the total compensation package offered by your employer and not contributing enough to get the full match is literally asking the employer for a salary reduction.

But, once the maximum match is reached, any other investing should be done elsewhere. Employer plans restrict you to limited investment choices and possibly deny you access to the money until you are fully vested or terminate employment. Also, many of these plans have fees that are greater than in the same (or comparable) investments you can buy on the open market. Finally, many of these plans are "cookie cutter," offering a preset investment portfolio that matches a retirement time horizon (10, 15, 20 years, etc.). This strategy may sound good until you compare the long-term performances and discover there is little or no significant difference between them. These retirement horizon plans also ignore the possibility that different employees have different needs and objectives beyond a simple estimate of years to retirement. Plan administrators offer little advice and even less periodic review to determine if financial objectives have changed—and the limited menu choices severely restrict how a person may invest.

But after making the maximum recommended plan contribution (enough to get the entire promised match), that sum may not be enough to adequately prepare for retirement. If so, where should you invest additional money? Fundamentally, there are two broad choices:

- Self-directed retirement plans that receive a current tax deduction (SEP, Individual IRA) but become fully taxable later upon receipt and a Required Minimum Distribution beginning at age 70½.
- Non-qualified, Tax-deferred (after-tax money) plans that while not offering a tax deduction this year, may offer important tax advantages later (e.g., Roth IRA, Non-Qualified Annuity, etc.).

The best recommendation depends on a number of factors, not the least of which is a person's current income tax bracket (note: rely on your total effective or net tax bracket rather than your top marginal tax bracket). It helps to know where your net tax falls within the tax bracket, so you know how much more income you can report without being taxed at a higher rate. Also, keep in mind that your tax bracket drops significant when your spouse dies—that is, a single person's bracket is much lower than a married couple, meaning your tax rate is higher at a lower amount of income resulting in higher taxes for you.

However, a big picture plan is not limited to minimizing your taxes this year. For example, deferring taxes today may result in a net reduction of current tax load but later could increase the tax load on your Social Security income for years. For example, compare two couples, both age 65, both retired and getting $60,000 in gross annual income:

- Couple A receives $20,000 from Social Security and $40,000 from a 401(k).
- Couple B receives $40,000 from Social Security and $20,000 from a 401(k).

Based on current code (2017), Couple A will report $51,100 of taxable income and Couple B will report $20,000.

Defined Benefit Plans also knows as “Pension Plans” accumulate money on a tax-deferred basis then converts that account into a permanent income for life at the point of retirement. While the Pension income is fully taxable at ordinary income rates, it has no tax consequences until the income begins and usually that is when you need a source of income to live through your retirement years.

MONEY SECRET: It’s not how much money you make that counts. It’s how much you get to keep.

Good tax planning is essential for financial planning. But simply calculating last year’s taxes offers no ability to make future adjustments that will reduce tax exposure. In 1934, Judge Learned Hand, writing for the 2nd Circuit Court said “*Anyone may so arrange his affairs that his taxes shall be as low as possible; he is not bound to choose that pattern which will best pay the Treasury; there is not even a patriotic duty to increase one’s taxes.*” Taking a proactive and forward-thinking approach to tax planning can increase how much you take home.

Tax planning is not about hiring a tax preparer or CPA to do your taxes and it’s certainly not about using do-it-yourself tax preparation software. Pro-active tax planning requires using the services of a tax planning professional (CPA, Enrolled Agent, Attorney, or Financial Advisor who gives *tax advice.*) A good tax planner will give you options that you can use to reduce your tax burden next year and for years to come.

CHAPTER 11
FINDING THE RIGHT ESTATE PLANNING ATTORNEY

People often say "*I've Got a Will and I've got a Power of Attorney so I'm set.*" But nothing could be farther from the truth. There is a real difference in the same types of documents people get from an Estate Planning Attorney specialist and a general practice attorney who also fixes parking tickets, handles divorce settlements, etc. More than just boiler plate legal documents, most retirees (seniors) face a number of other challenges not the least of which are Elder Law needs (Long Term Care concerns) and Asset Protection. Using an attorney who specializes in all these areas provides a far better result than using a generalist. Unfortunately, you won't know whether or not you have the documents you need until a crisis occurs, and at that point you may not be able to change what you've got. The documents you receive from an experienced Elder Law attorney will be very different from documents offered by most general practice attorneys. The distinction is significant because you need to know that your documents will work when you need them.

But planning is not just about the documents. It's also about the advice that comes with them. It's about the things your attorney puts into place that makes those documents work, and that's the #1 disconnect with people who think they've got it right but are wrong.

This begs the question, how can you tell the difference? If you go to an attorney and ask "*Can you do all these things?*" naturally they'll say "*Of course.*" But that doesn't necessarily mean they really do.

Sometimes people equate the size of the law firm with quality of advice but that's also not necessarily true. Many large law firms don't have attorneys on staff who specialize in Elder Law or Asset Protection. Also, the estate planning section of a large firm is commonly no larger than a small law firm that specializes in Estate Planning and/or Elder Law. The key is in knowing what to ask.

1. Inquire about the breadth of the lawyer's practice. An attorney who handles many different areas of law is a generalist and less likely to offer robust planning than someone who specializes in estate, trust, tax, and elder law.
2. Ask about expertise in all the critical areas: not just Will and Trust planning but also Elder Law including familiarity with Medicaid and veteran's benefits (even if you're not a veteran) and Asset Protection.
3. Ask about their Martindale-Hubbell® ratings. These peer-reviewed ratings that indicate an attorney's ethical standards and professional ability:
    a. **AV Preeminent** is highest rating available. It generally means that the attorney is within the top 1% of practitioners for that area of practice. The "v" denotes high ethical standards. An attorney without a "v" rating should be avoided.
    b. **AV** is the second highest rating denoting an experienced attorney in the top 10% of his/her peers.
    c. **BV Distinguished** is the next highest rating. It denotes a lawyer with experience that is above the average in the field.
    d. **BV Rated** designates an attorney who has met very high criteria of general ethical standing but is still below BV Distinguished.
    e. **Unrated** refers to lawyers who have not achieved these levels of peer review recognition.

4. Judge the initial session paying particular attention to where the attorney places emphasis. While basic documents are ultimately important, they should not be the first consideration. Good advice starts with a thorough understanding of family dynamics such as:
   - What are your needs, goals and circumstances?
   - What "skeletons are in your family closet?"
   - Do your children get along with each other? With you? With other family members?
   - Are your heirs savers or spenders? What about their spouses?
   - Are there any second (or more) marriages, etc.?
   - What are your hopes and fears? For yourself? Your heirs?
   - Does anyone have special needs or needs that are different, even inequitable from others?
   - Your net worth, how it grows and how it is allocated are certainly very important, but not as much as your family dynamics, your needs and desires and your individual circumstances.

Getting a handle on these concerns is more important than merely having a set of legal documents. In fact, those documents should be determined based on the answers to these (and many more) questions, not the other way around.

For example: Assume a family of modest means: One home worth $150,000 and a nest-egg of $300,000, mostly in a 401(k). The couple tells their attorney "*All I want is a simple plan that my spouse gets everything, then whatever is left after we're both gone, goes equally to the kids.*" Most lawyers will provide a "Sweetheart Plan" meaning a Will that leaves everything to the surviving spouse first and then bequeaths the rest equally distributed to the kids. And for many retirees, that is exactly the *wrong* plan.

Most seniors, even if they don't mention it in the first session, worry about outliving their money, about the potential need for Long Term Care and more. Basic "Sweetheart Plans" offer no provision for these needs. However, with a little more planning at modest cost, the same basic plan can also protect non-marital assets from in-laws, if marriages don't last or qualify for government assistance if needed for Nursing Care and so forth.

Commonly retirees claim "*My kids are doing better than us and say they don't care what happens to the assets.*" First of all, test this attitude. Threaten to bequeath the entire estate to the next-door neighbor and see how fast they change their minds or try to prove that you have lost your mind. Basically, there are only two possible choices to inherit your estate: those you wish and anyone else.

Next, it's important to recognize that there's a big difference between the plan on paper and the plan in real life and that difference is in how to actually *use* the plan. What's commonly misunderstood is that the key lies in the way property is held (titled and owned). An attorney that doesn't specifically talk about the best way to hold title cannot offer the best way to make the estate plan work. And sadly, many plans, even expensive plans with thick books of documents, completely fail, simply because property was improperly titled to meet the planning need.

For example, a couple jointly own title to their home, and their bank accounts and their investment accounts are owned Joint with Rights of Survivorship. These designations are easy to set up and cost nothing. After the first death, everything transfers seamlessly to the surviving spouse and everything seems fine. But, there is no provision for asset protection in the case of a Long Term Care need and suddenly the surviving spouse may be exposed to liability from creditors that were protected when the assets were jointly owned. Then after after the second spouse dies, everything goes into probate. As already discussed, probate can take a long time, cost a lot of money and invites a host of issues including claims from alleged heirs who feel they were unfairly cut out. Proper ownership considerations, both before and the first death are critical to the planning process. In other words, advance planning is proactive and effective. Planning after the fact is reactive and not effective.

MONEY SECRET: Get your legal advice from a specialist who understands more than just the preparation of legal documents. All retirees and seniors should get their estate planning advice and their documents from an experienced elder law attorney. Make sure you're your attorney actively networks with other professionals, including your financial planner, your CPA, etc. Estate Planning is a team effort. It may seem "complex" to consider all this now, but it's far more complex, and nightmarish to face the ramifications of inadequate or ineffective planning after-the-fact. Last, the worst mistake is to procrastinate about getting this planning done. No one likes to think about death or take the needed action, but families with no documents and no planning in place when the need arises face losing everything. Frankly, good estate planning is about "life planning"—your life and the family you leave behind, so get it done!

CHAPTER 12
PAYING FOR COLLEGE

There was a time when having a high school diploma was sufficient to get a decent job and earn a living wage. Back in the day, college was for people seeking professional status or advanced positions in the work force. Today, a college degree is the equivalent of yesterday's high school diploma and graduate school replaces what an undergraduate college degree did before.

This realization has two important financial implications:

1. It increases (by 4 years) the time you may need to financially support your children before they can strike out on their own.
2. It substantially increases the cost of getting your kids to a place of true independence.

Paying for college is not cheap and depending on the college of choice, could be a very substantial financial obligation. In 2016-2017, the average cost of attending a state-supported college was about $10,000 per year for qualified in-state students, $25,000 per year at those same schools for out-of-state residents and nearly $34,000 per year to most private colleges. However, there is tremendous disparity in the latter. For example, if your child wants to attend Yale the tuition is $50,000 per year and Harvard is $63,000 per year. Now multiply those costs by four years and then multiply that by the number of children you have.

Saving for college should start long before your child is a senior in high school. For any college savings plan to be effective, the plan needs time for the investment to compound and grow. Albert Einstein famously said "*The greatest force in the universe is compound interest.*" And in the case of planning for college, that's certainly true, but compounding only works when you start early. Remember, it's called "*time* and compounding."

Any long-term investment plan has the capability of being used to pay for college. However, open investments, if successful, will have the gains taxed upon liquidation and may also generate taxable income while growing. However, there are two types of tax-advantaged college savings plans:

- Education Savings Accounts (ESAs or Coverdell Plans)
- 529 Plans.

Both offer the advantage of tax-deferred growth and tax-free access if used to pay for qualified costs of higher education (tuition, etc.). But the differences stop there. ESAs limit the annual contribution per beneficiary to $2000 per year up to age 18. Even if you started when the kid was born and earned a whopping 7% annual return, every year, that amounts to a little more than $74,750; barely enough to pay for four years of college without considering the inevitable impact of inflation. In addition, based on your income, the allowable contribution amount may be less than $2000 per year.

A 529 Plan permits an initial deposit of up to five times the annual gift allowance which (in 2017) is $14,000. In other words, you could make an initial deposit of as much as $70,000. Don't have that much? Don't worry, it can be less and contributions may continue from the start until the time the student is ready to go. Also, contributions can be made by anyone. In addition, 529 Plans are somewhat more flexible in what they consider a qualified expense.

529 Plans do differ by state so a detailed discussion of these is best left to a financial planning professional familiar with them. You can in-

vest in any state's 529 plan, but depending on your state of residence, may or may not be subject to state income tax on receipt of the money if you use the plan of another state than where you live.

Regardless of whether you use a 529, Coverdell, or simply plan to use "regular money," once you have the money to pay for college, the next challenge is to reduce how much *you* or your child must pay. This can be accomplished in one of several ways.

1. **Scholarships**. Fundamentally scholarships come from three broad sources:
   a. **Talent-based Scholarships.** These come directly from the college your child will attend and can either be academic or athletic.
      - **Academic**—To qualify, the student must meet very high standards of academic promise—grades, test scores, etc. sufficient for the school to want to enroll that student—potentially more than the student wants to attend that school.
      - **Athletic**—To qualify, the student must offer the school an athletic ability the school sees as beneficial for its sports programs, especially those which generate revenue for the school (football, basketball, etc.). However, if the student gets injured and can no longer play, the scholarship can be lost.
   b. **Need-based Scholarships.** These are scholarships and grants awarded to students with specific financial need. For example, a student may qualify by being classified as an Independent Student because of one of the following:
      - Age 24 or older
      - A military veteran, or currently serves on active duty in the armed forces
      - An orphan
      - A ward of the court or in foster care when 13 years or older
      - Married
      - Have legal dependents other than a spouse

- Is a graduate student or professional student
- Is an emancipated minor or in legal guardianship
- Is homeless
- Is a student for whom a financial aid administrator documents independence for other reasons.

c. **Outside Scholarships.** There are literally thousands of private scholarships available, from churches, to charities, to private clubs and civic organizations, even places of employment. Many are esoteric but readily available, sometimes merely for the asking. Hunting these down takes effort and persistence, but under the right circumstances, can be dove-tailed to pay for the majority if not entirety of the cost of education. There are also Vocational Rehabilitation Funds for students with a certain documented learning disability: ADD, ADHD, etc. These programs are administered by the counties primarily to help its citizens get into the workforce, but where the intended occupation requires a college degree, they will help finance the education.

2. **Grants** (such as the Pell Grant) are federal subsidized sources of money, primarily for students with financial need. Unlike loans, grants do not require repayment. Some colleges and universities that have large endowments will offer grants to need-based students rather than loans.

3. **College Loans** are popular ways to pay for college but represent a growing financial crisis in the United States. According to a report by the New York Federal Reserve, by year-end 2016, the total student loan debt in the country was $1.31 Trillion with an average delinquency or default rate of 11.2%, and default doesn't mean the student can avoid paying it. Student loans cannot be eliminated in bankruptcy and student loans can be garnished from your wages under Federal law. Hence, unpaid student loans will follow you forever until they are paid or until your death. For many graduates and those who drop out, their student loans can be as much or more than a mortgage

payment. In those cases, the college loan put the recipient financially way behind their peers without those loan payments and perhaps even behind someone who went to technical school or straight into the work force from high school.

4. **Attending a college that is more affordable.** As already seen, state-supported schools can be less expensive than private but only for qualified in-state students. However, sometimes private schools can be less expensive than public. Originally, private schools were for the wealthy and elite and public schools arose to cater to the higher education needs of the masses. More recently, however, those roles have reversed. Today, public institutions, especially major universities are flooded with applications, including by students from high net worth families and students with superlative academic or athletic credentials. As a result, these universities must reject as many, if not more than they accept, simply because they lack the capacity to support them. Conversely, more and more, private schools, especially the smaller ones, must create new strategies to attract students. One of those inventions was the institutional grant. These are grants awarded in addition to any scholarships earned and any federal or state grants the student may qualify for. Public institutions don't offer this. Therefore, even though the published tuition may be more at a private school, the actual tuition paid can be less. However, some costs are constant: the cost of living (housing, food) for example. The big variable is in the cost of tuition and this is where institutional grants can make a big difference.

   Another less expensive alternative is to attend a community college or technical school or local college for the first two years while living at home. This provides a huge savings compared to attending a college or university away from home. Often, in-state schools will accept community/technical college credits without any issues. However, it is important to check what credits will be accepted by the college of your choice because some schools, particularly private schools, will not accept the transfer credits.

FAFSA—Free Application for Federal Student is the first place to start. Often parents fail to complete this form because they *"make too much"* but don't make that assumption. Because the FASFA form is the one form used for everything, not just Pell Grants which are for the economically disadvantaged. But be careful. There is a commercial site that sells the FAFSA form (fafsa.com) that is not affiliated with the real website https://fasfa.ed.gov. Logic alone should be the guide here but clearly too many people are tricked. However, the FAFSA form is called the Free Application. You don't pay for something if it's free. Worse is that the commercial website asks for all your private information: Social Security number, your past two years of tax returns; everything the government website would ask for, except that you just gave it to a commercial entity. It doesn't matter that they say your information is protected. You just made it public. Basically, any website that asks for money to apply for a scholarship should be avoided.

MONEY SECRET: Adhere to the following sequence of steps for college financing:

1. Set up your personal college funding program early; when your child is still in diapers.
2. Complete the FASFA Form at https://fasfa.ed.gov
3. Then, during the student's senior year in high school, identify and apply for as many Outside Scholarships and Grants as possible. Treat this as an after-school job.
4. Next, seek Institutional Scholarships and Grants. Meet with and talk to the prospective colleges' financial aid officers. They can provide guidance and advice, not just in terms of what the institution may provide, but also offer suggestions of where to go after additional money. Where institutional financial aid is specifically for attending the school offering it, outside aid is generally not for a particular school.
5. Then, if necessary, apply for Federal Direct Loans.
6. Finally, if still necessary, apply for Private Loans. Parents and others should avoid co-signing any student loan.

CHAPTER 13
HEALTH IS WEALTH

Health insurance and other health care costs are less if you're healthy, but there's a lot more to it. You've got to be healthy to enjoy life. An old saying goes "*You can spend all your health to get wealth but then you have to spend all your wealth to regain your health.*"

The bottom line is that anyone with a significant life-limiting health problem would give all their wealth to regain good health for the rest of their lifetime, but good health doesn't work that way.

We're bombarded with advice on how to get and stay healthy. These include the foods to eat (or don't eat), the best supplements to take and the ideal exercise program to follow. Often that advice is contradictory and changes regularly. (Think sugar vs. sugar substitutes, butter vs. margarine, salt vs. salt substitutes, fat vs. non-fat foods, red meat, etc.)

Despite being largely overweight, compared with third world countries, Americans, on average, are healthy people. The key then is to stay healthy. But as we age, our healthful habits change. We eat more and exercise less.

Financially, healthy living is more than just staying healthy.

For example, if a 25 year-old who smokes just one pack of cigarettes a day instead didn't smoke and invested the cigarette money in a conservative fund, by age 70, that non-smoker would have well over $1 Million in a savings account (and wouldn't be coughing).

One of the common admonitions about healthful eating is to avoid white sugar. That starts with the consumption of soft drinks. Now this book is about "Money Secrets" so we're not going to lecture you about drinking too much soda, except that buying soft drinks, especially at restaurants has financial consequences.

Restaurants love to sell soft drinks because their profit margin is greater than anything else they sell. Thus, a night out with a family of four, at $2.50 a piece, the soda alone adds $10 to the total tab. At that rate, the total annual cost of dinner out once a week is $520 just for soda for family dinner night! All that and never mind the amount of sugar you just consumed with all those drinks. Conversely a glass of water (perhaps with a wedge of lemon) is not only healthier but saves you a lot of money. Recently we saw a promotion in a big chain grocery store: buy one 2 Liter bottle of soda for $1.99 or buy 5 for $5. Most people would opt for the $5 purchase because they're "saving money." However, that person just bought 10 liters of soda; over 2½ gallons and it's likely they'll drink that faster than had they just bought one bottle, and soon be back to purchase another 5 bottles (the grocery store knows and is counting on this). Not only is the shopper now spending a lot more on soda (net) than initially intended, there is a tremendous increase of otherwise unintended sugar consumption.

Some people focus on shopping at health food stores because the food is "Organic." But that term means the food was grown without pesticides. Regardless of whether that makes the food more desirable, it's still the same food and in some cases, biologically makes absolutely no difference to the overall nutritional content, nor does it have anything to do with what happens to the food after it is cooked. And not everything at a health food store is healthy. The key to healthy eating is being balanced and varied, and making simple choices. It's not necessary to always purchase expensive specialty items to prepare healthy meals nor is it necessary to load up on supplemental vitamins and minerals to replace what is supposedly not in basic food. So much of what diminishes the nutritional content of food is processing. However, food—especially fruits and vegetables that are mass produced by distant super farms—lack the full nutritional value of locally produced items simply because they are not permitted the time to "vine ripen." In addition, because these foods don't taste as good, they require more additives at the time of preparation to improve their overall taste and quality. The simplest and least expensive alternative is to patronize local farmers at farmer's markets. Not only is that food better quality, better tasting, and supports the local economy, it is often less expensive because buying directly from the grower eliminates the cost of transportation and all the other middlemen.

Another key ingredient in healthful living is avoiding stress. Stress triggers the "Fight or Flight" response which is a hormonal response that releases adrenalin. Adrenalin is important to adapting to emergency situations, but when it's preset too much, it's problematic. Exercise—even informal, casual activity, tends to relieve stress.

Health and wealth coincide in several ways:

1. At the job—people who are not in good health do not perform their best and are less productive than those who are. Lack of productivity has the potential to cost promotions. Being out due to sickness frequently has even direr financial consequences.
2. Top tips—stay away from the "whites" avoid too much white flour, white sugar and dairy. Everything is in moderation.
3. Exercise! Regular exercise "fixes" a lot of healthful problems and good health is good economics
4. Avoid energy drinks. They're filled with tons of sugar and high caffeine that does not give you "energy." Essentially they induce you into a hyper-alert state with short-term solutions by altering the body's biochemistry. They're a step below the recreational use of drugs so you can feel better, get high, stay awake all night and go to sleep after.

5. We're over-dependent on pills and supplements to "fix things." Rather than use artificial supplements to "fix" problems (which they really don't), find out the reason for the problem and address the underlying cause. Superficially treating symptoms merely masks what's wrong.

MONEY SECRET: You don't need us to tell you the solutions; your doctor tells (or should tell) you every year. Beyond that, life is all about choices, be they health or financial, or both. The choices you make today, help determine your future, health wise and financially. Poor financial choices result in not enough money for your retirement years; poor health choices often result (but not always) in diabetes, heart disease, COPD, and other life limiting ailments. Make good choices for your yourself and your family.

CHAPTER 14
SMALL BUSINESS OWNERSHIP

Owning your own business is the American Dream. Many people follow that path but once you make that decision, or even if you already have, the next question to ask is "*What structure should my business take?*" There are several distinct arrangements, each with advantages and liabilities, mostly having to do with the tax status of the business.

Sole Proprietorship. This is the simplest form of business. It requires no formal business model and no filing with the state. Any profits or losses you have are directly reported on your individual income tax return. You must withhold and pay FICA tax (Social Security and Medicare Tax) which (currently) is 15.3%. There are two specific liabilities with Sole Proprietorships.

1. Because there is no formal structure, sole proprietors often fail to keep adequate records of the business activities. Because of this, if there's an audit, they may have a difficult time demonstrating to an IRS auditor what was and wasn't reported.
2. Sole Proprietorships offer no protection from claims of liability. If there is a complaint that generates a lawsuit, the business owner's personal (non-business) assets are at risk.

Partnership. With several variants, these are non-incorporated businesses in which two or more people own and run the business.

Ownership may be equal or unequal depending on particulars. What partnerships offer is a division of ownership and operational duties. It's a simple and effective way to combine resources from different people with different areas of expertise. Depending on how a partnership is organized and your role in the partnership, some limited liability may be available. However, as a general rule, partnerships offer no liability protection for each and every partner's personal assets from a claim against any one partner.

General Partnership. In this arrangement, all the partners have voting rights and the right to exercise control as well as shared liability if any partner gets sued.

Limited Partnership. Here, only the Managing (or General) Partners have voting rights, control rights, and personal liability. The Limited Partners, while having a financial interest in the partnership, do not have control rights and have no outside personal liability for actions of the partnership. Limited partners can lose only their investment in the partnership.

Tax-wise, all partnerships are "Pass-Through" entities. In a Pass-Through, the partnership pays no income tax itself. Rather, it records income and expenses, computes net profit or loss, files a Partnership Tax Return with a K-1 to each Partner which is passed on to the personal tax return (Line 12 on Form 1040) of each partner proportional to their ownership stake.

Limited Liability Company (LLC). Functionally, an LLC resembles a Partnership, but when formed, you can choose to be taxed as a Corporation, a Sub-S Corporation or as a Partnership. If no selection is made, the default tax category is a Partnership. An LLC can be a Member-Managed entity or a Manager-Managed entity. That decision is made when you file your Articles of Organization and create your Operating Agreement. A Member-Managed LLC works like a true Partnership where the Partners together make important decisions for the Company. There are two major differences with a true Partnership:

1. the LLC Members have limited liability (which is a good thing), but an LLC member (normally) cannot quit the LLC at any time
2. a Partner can resign from a Partnership without limitation (this can be good or bad depending upon the situation).

Most LLC's are created as Manager-Managed entities. The LLC still enjoys limited liability (just like a Corporation), but the Members select the Manager or Managers, and then the Managers operate the entity (not unlike a Corporation that selects a President or CEO to run the every-day operations of the Company). Unless the LLC is taxed as a regular Corporation, the LLC is a Pass-Through entity for income tax purposes (like a Partnership or Sub-S Corporation). This means the entity files a tax return, but pays no tax. Instead it gives each Member a K-1 for that member to report the LLC's profit or loss specific to that Member's interest on his/her personal tax return.

A Limited Liability Company is an entity authorized by state statute and must be filed and registered with the Secretary of State (in most states; some states it is filed in a different department), including pay initial filing fees, followed by annual fees. The LLC must get a separate FEIN (Federal Tax ID Number) to be able to file Federal, State, and local taxes.

Unlike a Partnership, an LLC may have only one Member, who may or may not act as the Manager. The Manager of an LLC is not required to be an owner (member). Also unlike a Partnership, both the Managers and Members of an LLC may enjoy significant personal protection from liability. A Partner who gets sued because of the act of another Partner or employee has their entire investment at risk as well as all his/her personal assets. A Member of an LLC has only their LLC investment at risk, and that investment is secondarily protected in "exclusive remedy" states where a "Charging Order" is given as the exclusive remedy for judgment creditors of the LLC.

In an "exclusive remedy" state, if a properly structured LLC gets sued and loses, the successful plaintiff (judgment creditor) does not receive an award of cash. Instead he gets a "Charging Order" meaning the creditor is now treated as a non-voting Member. As such, if the LLC generates profit *and* makes distributions of that profit to its members, the creditor stands in the shoes of the member and gets the proportionate share. However, the Manager has full discretion to distribute profits or not. Any time profit is generated, even if there is no actual distribution, that profit is reported to all Members as a taxable event (Form K-1). This means that, at the sole discretion of the Manager, the plaintiff could receive a tax bill but no money as a result of winning the lawsuit. The creditor has no say in the management of the LLC and cannot require the LLC to dissolve in order to reach the assets owned by the LLC, or even demand that the profits be distributed. In addition, with no opportunity for a large cash award, the plaintiff's attorney will have to work pro bono (for free) or on a fee-for-service basis (very expensive). As a result, lawsuits against LLC's in these jurisdictions are often avoided making creditors discount their claims so that a settlement can be reached that is more favorable to the LLC. Of course, this is where having a good umbrella policy works wonders.

S-Corporation (S-Corp). This is a formally incorporated business entity. S-Corps are filed and registered with Secretary of State (in most states), receive a separate Tax ID Number (FEIN) and must file a separate income tax return (due March 15, not April 15) with K-1's being given to each stockholder. Like most LLC's, S-Corps are Pass-through entities so profits (and losses) of the company appear on the individual return of the company's owner(s). While Sub-S Corporations enjoy limited liability protections for its stockholders, corporations do not enjoy the benefits of "charging orders' for its judgment creditors.

Compared with an LLC, there is potential tax advantage associated with an S-Corp over an LLC. With an LLC, 100% of the profit generated by the company is subject to FICA Tax (Social Security and Medicare) up to the stated maximum FICA withholding limit (first $127,200 of net income in 2017). The FICA tax consists of 7.65% from the employee plus 7.65% from the employer but in the case of an S-Corp, the owner (by pass-through) is both, meaning the individual tax withholding is 15.3% in addition to ordinary income tax. Conversely, an S-Corp only pays FICA on the salary paid to employees, including the owner. Therefore, an S-Corp owner who takes less than the maximum withholding limit will save FICA on the difference, and the S-Corp owner has direct, discretionary access to all the money in the corporation's account. However, the IRS requires the owner of an S-Corp to be paid a "fair wage." Thus, a profitable S-Corp that generates well in excess of the maximum withholding limit cannot pay the owner an annual salary of $1. Also, it is important to remember that FICA is the basis of a future Social Security income benefit. Taking a minimum salary to minimize FICA exposure may cost significant Social Security income in retirement. Ideally, an S-Corp owner should take just enough income to achieve the maximum future Social Security benefit, but not more unless required to meet the reasonable salary test. While nobody can make pinpoint future predictions, a good financial planner or tax planner can help project reasonable levels.

LLC's can elect to file income taxes as an S-Corp, thereby enjoying the benefits of both an LLC and an S-Corp. Even though both entities enjoy limited liability for its owners, each should protect itself with good liability umbrella insurance coverage as well as other professional liability insurance and workman's compensation insurance.

C Corporation (C-Corp). By definition, a C-Corp is any corporation that is taxed separately from its owners. Like LLCs and S-Corps, C-Corps are filed with the Secretary of State and receive a separate FEIN. But, the income tax calculation, including the tax rates is very different for a C-Corp, and commonly larger.

One of the common complaints about C-Corp taxation is called "Double Taxation." This occurs when a C-Corp pays a dividend (a profit-sharing payment to shareholders). Because the company must report (and pay) tax on its net profits as business income, then the owners (stockholders) must report (and pay) tax on the dividend from the corporation as personal income; that Dividend gets taxed twice, once by the corporation, and then again by the stockholders resulting in "Double Taxation." However, only Dividends get "Double Taxed." Note that shareholders who receive a Dividend gets individually taxed on the payment, but does not personally pay the taxes of the company or have liability for the corporations taxes.

A C-Corp cannot transfer losses to the owner's personal return; hence many start-ups choose an S-Corp formation so that losses can go to the owners' personal income tax return. Corporation profits are generally taxed at a higher schedule, with exceptions for companies with small profits that have much lower rates.

A large C-Corp, especially if very profitable, can do far more benefit planning for its employees, including key employees which are deductible expenses to the corporation; similar benefits are not available to an S-Corp or an LLC.

Business Structure Conclusion—Ultimately the best choice of business structure depends on a lot of variables, including the probability of losses in the first years, how much control the founder desires, how big the company will be, how many employees it will have, whether it is to be held privately or is intended to go public, if it will exist entirely within one city or state, or have international connections or investors, etc.

Data Tracking—After determining the Business Structure, the next biggest concern, and one that is perhaps the most common mistake, is inadequate or improper tracking: keeping records of profits, losses and receipts for all expenses including business mileage. But more than simple record keeping is the need for an understanding of how to move money in and out of a small business account, asking the right legal questions, and understanding the structure of the business, how it works and what its limitations are.

1. Day-to-day data tracking can identify deductions that are forgotten, in the aggregate are under-estimated, or even not realized by the business owner.
2. In an audit, the IRS will require physical evidence of the deduction to document not only its legitimacy but also the claimed value.

Mileage Deductions—Another big and common mistake made by small business owners relates to vehicle deductions. A vehicle used for business is subject to a deduction under one of two methods:

- Standard mileage deduction
- Actual expense (receipts)

The preferred choice depends on the type of vehicle and how much it's driven. For example, data and experience show that unless a vehicle gets less than15 MPG, mileage deductions are usually preferable, especially if the vehicle is driven more than 9000 miles per year *for business* use. Commuting between home and work is not deductible. Thus, if the vehicle is seldom or never driven except to and from work, an actual expense deduction may be better. But, businesses with a lot of business vehicle usage (e.g., realtors), are substantially benefitted by the mileage deduction. Conversely, the older a vehicle is, the more maintenance and repair it requires and the more an expense deduction may be beneficial. However, there is a trap. If an expense deduction is taken in the first year, then only expense deductions are permitted thereafter. Conversely, if a mileage deduction is taken in the first year, the business owner may switch back and forth in subsequent years.

Vehicle Depreciation—A vehicle, whether new or pre-owned, that is bought for business can be depreciated. Also, a bonus depreciation is available, but for new vehicles only. This bonus depreciation allows a much greater amount of the vehicle to be written off in the first year, but with a caveat: if the vehicle is financed and the terms of the loan are longer than the ownership (e.g. a 5-year loan on a vehicle kept 3 years), this negatively impacts how much may be depreciated from the subsequent new vehicle. Conversely, larger vehicles (think large SUV's and trucks or larger) over a certain tonnage offer the business owner the ability to deduct the full cost of the vehicle in the first year; smaller vehicles don't get this quick write-off.

Home Office Deductions—Businesses that operate out of the owner's residence may be able to deduct a portion of the household expenses (utilities, etc.) and depreciate the square footage of the office (relative to the home) as a Schedule C Home Office deduction. Again, careful record-keeping is essential and caution is warranted.

1. Many in-home businesses are more "hobbies" than actual businesses and a home office deduction, especially if large in proportion to the amount of business income reported, can raise red flags with the IRS. Essentially, if an in-home business is not a legitimate business, operating as such and generating a profit commensurate with a real, commercial business, taking a Home Office Deduction may result in more harm than good. Red flags mean that your deduction make an IRS audit more likely.
2. Selling a home from which a Home Office Deduction was taken, may expose the owner to a second, unforeseen tax liability. Currently, a home owner who lives in a house at least six months of the year for two of the past five years enjoys a significant exemption on the capital appreciation from the sale of the home: $250,000 per spouse (meaning $500,000 for a couple). But Home Office deductions may reduce that allowable exemption. The good news is that unless the home has appreciated considerably and the home office deduction is far greater than the average (8% per year average), the total of Home Office deductions will not likely exceed the realized capital appreciation on the home and not disrupt the ability to deduct the gains. The math can be complicated so if you take this deduction, have an accountant prepare your tax returns.

MONEY SECRET: The decision to open and run a business is an important one that requires considerable thought. It starts with a careful determination of the best way to structure the business, specifically with regard to control, taxation and limitations on liability. Next, good record keeping is essential to efficiently run the business and maintain maximum tax efficiency.

It's easy to file papers with the Secretary of State to form a company. However, most people who do this without professional help fail to do anything other than to file the initial papers. This means you failed to do what is legally required to maintain the company's limited liability and/

or failed to timely make your tax elections. Getting good advice saves you time and money in both the short-term run and long-term.

Finally knowing how to determine the best sources of tax deductions or how and when to take them can offer substantial advantages to any business owner. These things are best obtained in direct consultation with legal and tax planning professionals.

CHAPTER 15
"NEW WORLD" ECONOMICS

For investors, major changes in the tax code could have a dramatic impact.

The current tax code (2017) includes five progressive tax brackets where everyone with sufficient income starts at the lowest rate (10%) and based on income, steps up thereafter. In other words, everyone (2017), regardless of total income or net worth pays the same tax rate on the first tier of income ($0 to $9525 if filing single; $0 to $19,050 if filing joint). Only the very wealthy ever pay at the highest tax bracket and then only on the income above that threshold.

However, recent proposed changes to tax law seek to eliminate deductions, including some of the standard deductions to which everyone is currently entitled. There are several economic implications (good and bad depending on your status) that would result.

1. Most low-income people will pay more in income tax and the wealthy will pay less.
2. Taxes ultimately pay for the business of running the country; for our infrastructure which includes transportation, safety, services, etc. Any tax reduction that results in less net income for the treasury increases the national deficit. That means tax changes are, or at least should be, net revenue neutral if not greater. When a country runs a deficit,

without increasing net (not gross) revenue for that nation's treasury, there is no chance of having that deficit shrink.

The terms "Debt" and "Deficit" are commonly tossed around like political footballs often without an understanding of what they mean or how they differ.

Deficit is the annual difference between government revenue (income) and government spending.

Debt is the total amount of money the government owes, including the accumulation of past deficits minuses surpluses. However, despite the popular analogy, government debt is not like a credit card that's been "maxed to the limit." Rather the U.S. debt is sold to investors, foreign and domestic, in the form of government bonds: Treasury Bills (T-Bills), Treasury Notes and Savings Bonds. Note that, by definition, Bonds are a "*Debt* Investment" (stocks are equity) and the United States has a long history of issuing debt to pay for national expenses. For example, to pay for World War II, the United States issued "War Bonds." In fact, this process dates back to 1790 when the fledgling government (as a nation, the United States officially began in 1789) issued debt to pay for the Revolutionary War and the establishment of the nation. Let us pray we don't find ourselves in a war with North Korea—the result would be horrific and the cost in lives and money would be profound.

3. Municipal Bond issuance, especially to high income investors who buy a lot, could be affected. One advantage of Municipal Bonds is that they're not subject to federal income tax. But reducing the top marginal tax brackets reduces the desirability of the bonds. The consequence would likely be that the issuers raise the coupon (interest) rates being offered which, in turn, reduces the economic effectiveness of them to the issuing municipalities. In other words, cities and counties would have to offer more interest on their bond to get investors to buy them; that extra interest will an additional cost that local taxpayers must bear which puts pressure on state and local taxes to increase.

4. Historically tax reductions are balanced by eliminating deductions. But most "tax cuts" are net revenue neutral meaning when Congress gives something (tax cuts) they take something else back (eliminate deductions) so the total amount of taxes paid remains unchanged. The current Tax Reform proposal being discussed today is not even close to tax neutral. Conservatively, it is projected to increase the deficit by One Trillion Dollars (or more) over the next 10 years. Such a result has the potential to generate a stock market correction, or recession, or both. Additional National Debt will also increase interest rates for good and bad—good for savers and bad for borrowers.
5. When Congress creates an annual budget, it earmarks money to spend on all the known and reasonably expected (imagined) financial needs. What's not fully accounted for are unexpected events. For example, on August 25, 2017, Hurricane Harvey pounded the Texas Gulf Coast, becoming the costliest single natural disaster in US history. The bill was estimated at $190 Billion. Two weeks later, on September 10, Hurricane Irma struck Florida causing damage that exceeded another $100 Billion. Much of the clean-up and recovery cost will be paid by FEMA. That will add to the 2017 Deficit, projected at $440 Billion before the storms.
6. For over three decades, there been a debate as to whether tax cuts (to the wealthy) stimulate additional growth that then "trickles down" to the common man or whether increasing net income to the middle and lower classes stimulated buying. The theory is that by reducing the tax burden on the wealthy and for corporations, the extra money enjoyed will be used to capitalize new business growth adding new jobs to the economy. However research by the International Monetary Fund, as well as a lot of others, have shown this economic theory, first popularized 1980's, is not correct. In a study of more than 150 countries, the researchers found that for every 1% income increase the top 20% of income earners enjoyed, the annual rate of growth in the country shrunk by 0.1% over the next five years. Conversely, for every 1% income increase received by the lowest 20% of earners,

the economy grew by 0.4%. Other economic research has shown that only a third of the revenue lost to tax cuts is recovered by stimulating trickle-down growth. Consequently, this economic strategy generates an increase in borrowing (issuance of government bonds) and thereby an increase in the national debt as well as the deficit. The current conservative estimate for the tax overhaul legislation is One Trillion Dollars over 10 years added to the country's deficit.

Conversely, compared with the wealthy, lower and middle-income earners typically spend more when they have more. This predicts a greater national economic benefit when the lower income earners have the lowest tax loads.

7. Contrary to popular belief, the government does not run the economy. That's up to individual businesses and consumers. At the large-scale ("macroeconomic") level, the general economic sentiment of these forces drives how the economy responds. There are long-term forces far more important than what the federal government does. For example, we're an aging society and that impacts a lot of businesses, including reduced employee turnover, changing benefits structure as well as societal impacts such as on things like Social Security, Medicare and Medicaid.
8. Another economic concern is technological unemployment. These days, technology is becoming so adept at doing what it does that by mid-century as many as half of the work-force jobs today may be done by machines. This, in turn, predicts a significant impact in education because a lot more people will be coming back to college later in life to change their careers. A possible consequence of this is a resurgence of cottage industry. Increasingly, people are abandoning the corporate environment for a return to small businesses that they can control.
9. Finally, markets and interest rates respond to each other. In the years since the end of the Great Recession of 2008, the markets have risen dramatically and in the eyes of many, too fast. As a long-term trend, when the prices of stocks rise faster than the value of the underlying

companies, stock prices become over-inflated and that predicts a correction (a decline in the markets). Generally, markets respond most dramatically to future events and the greater the excess in company valuations, the more sensitive those potential market shocks can be, especially when those events are unexpected. Interest rates in turn respond as well. If interest rates increase, that change would benefit investors seeking to exit the markets as they fall. At the same time, rising interest rates would negatively impact borrowers.

MONEY SECRET: Large scale economic (Macroeconomics) changes are impacted more by business and consumer activity than government intervention. However, the way in which businesses and consumers respond to large scale changes in tax structure, including proposed changes, can significantly impact the economics of individuals (Microeconomics). Knee jerk reactions seldom provide advantageous results, particularly when decisions are made on the basis of inaccurate or incomplete information. Prudence and a long-term view which includes solid planning, provides the best way to weather economic storms. Unfortunately, seniors don't have the luxury of long term planning or waiting out a rebound in the market and must spend from savings each month.

Regardless of what changes Congress will make to the tax code, now or in the future, any major change will benefit some and harm others. For example, the current tax change proposals, if adopted, will result in a loss of popular personal tax deductions or exemptions as well as (presumably) some corporate tax loopholes will be plugged. We are confident that if the changes currently being discussed are implemented, the nation's debt and deficit will likely rise dramatically over the next ten years. Such a result will increase the tax burden on our children and grandchildren. We also know that tax changes that increase interest rates will be good for savers and bad for borrowers.

Clearly, some taxpayers will benefit and others will not. We pray that any major tax change will bring with it good news and positive economic activity and outcomes in the country. But it is wise to be skeptical with anything done in Washington where Congress runs on money and campaign contributions fuels Congress. With any major tax change, some people will know their personal tax outcome in advance and the rest will learn the result after filing their first tax return.

CHAPTER 16
INSURANCE FOR INCOME

We insure all our important possessions: car and home, even specialty personal items such as jewelry. We insure our health and use insurance to protect loved ones from the financial hardship of a premature death. Insurance is the foundation of all asset protection. This then begs the question, "Why not insure your retirement income?"

Other than life and health, perhaps more important than material possessions is the need for a living income that cannot be outlived.

It's perhaps ironic that people infrequently question the strength and stability of their car and home insurance company. Even less frequently do folks inquire about their bank or brokerage firm, but people become very resistant, sometimes even paranoid about insurance companies as soon as financial products are mentioned.

How safe are insurance companies?

Many people are surprised to learn that because of insurance law and regulation, insurance products are actually the safest form of money there is. With that said, some insurance companies are stronger than others, and there is merit in considering the strength of an insurance company before purchasing that company's product. However, the level of minimum security imposed by state regulators is so tight it's a bit like worrying if you plunged off a 59 story vs. a 60 story building, would the outcome be any different. In short, insurance companies are very strong financial institutions that are highly regulated and very safe.

Reserve Minimums—Most everyone is familiar with FDIC insurance on banks. Started by the Glass-Steagall Act of 1933, FDIC was established to insure bank deposits up to stated limits (previously $100,000 per depositor per institution, increased to $250,000 after the Great Recession). Essentially FDIC (Federal Deposit Insurance Corporation) is an insurance company chartered by the federal government, but run independently. From its inception, not one depositor has lost a cent of FDIC insured money. That makes insured bank deposits very safe. Despite that, insurance contracts have even greater safety than FDIC insured accounts. The reason relates to minimum reserve requirements.

A reserve requirement is the minimum amount of cash that an institution must have on hand to cover its obligations. As of January 2017, the mandated Reserve Requirement for Federal Reserve Banks (and FDIC-insured banks) is 0% for the first $15.5 Million in assets, 3% for assets totaling between $15.5 and $115.1 Million and 10% for assets above $115.1 Million. Thus, a large bank with $1 Billion in total assets has a net reserve of $91.49 Million (approximately 9.5%). The rest is a promissory note ultimately secured by FDIC insurance. But FDIC does not have enough cash in its own bank to insure every insured bank in the country. According to www.fdic.gov, FDIC's own reserves amount to 1.35%, or $13.5 Million to insure that $1 Billion with the bank. The rest is protected by the federal government's ability to declare a bail-out.

Conversely, insurance companies are required to maintain a minimum 100% reserves. Thus, a $1 Billion insurance company must literally have ready access to not less than $1 Billion in cash. Moreover, most insurance companies carry excess above reserves as a cushion. In fact, the independent ratings agencies (e.g., A.M. Best) do not assign top ratings to companies whose assets are barely above the reserve minimum. In addition, insurance companies are reinsured, meaning they purchase insurance policies against excess claims. If one insurance company experiences uncharacteristically high claims, the reinsurance company pays a portion of those claims, thereby mitigating the original company's financial risk. The potential for extraordinary high claims normally arise in the casualty insurance markets (think hurricanes, floods or major fires) and those companies tend to re-insure most of their claims risk.

Finally, insurance is regulated by the states, each of which requires all companies within their jurisdiction to contribute into a state insurance reserve pool. This sum serves to back up the states (and all insurance contracts therein) in case an insurer does become insolvent.

Therefore, every state requires an annual financial audit of every carrier in its jurisdiction. Thus, an insurance company admitted to all 50 states plus the District of Columbia must undergo a financial audit the equivalent of once a week. And, if the system breaks down, the states are on the hook. Imagine a situation where if the burglar gets away, the police go to jail. As safe as banks are, nothing in the banking industry compares with insurance regulation. (Note. The fixed annuity contract comment "Not insured by FDIC" that worries some people, is irrelevant. FDIC insures only banks so saying an insurance product is not FDIC insured is like saying your new Toyota is not made with genuine Ford parts.)

Pooled Risk—Insurance companies are able to accomplish what they do because of pooled risk and the law of large numbers. Simply, this means that by issuing hundreds of thousands of policies, the insurer has a very high reliability of being able to statistically predict the likelihood of paying a claim in any given year. For example, if you toss a fair coin, you know that the result will (eventually) be half heads and half tails. But it's possible the first 6 or 8 tosses will be the same thing. That does not invalidate the odds. Rather it means the sample size was too small. Repeat that coin flip a hundred thousand times and the results will be 50/50. Pooled risk means that for every policy which requires a claim, there are many, many policies which don't.

Why insure income? Retirement is a time of life when a person lives off what they accomplished in the past, including Social Security. The

Social Security income a person receives at retirement is derived directly from the amount of tax paid in while working (the FICA Tax). Technically, Social Security payments are a form of an annuity meaning "annual income" derived from a common source. Once earned, those income payments are guaranteed for life. However, for most retirees, Social Security income payments alone are not enough. In truth, Social Security was never designed to be a person's sole source of retirement income.

Too often, people underestimate the true cost of living in retirement. For example, assume a married couple both age 60, eating three meals a day that average just $10 each. That's $60 per day. (We know that people don't eat like this, but the illustration of spending is valid.) Over the course of a year, they spend $21,900 in food. If they live to age 90, they've spent $657,000 on just food. That ignores inflation. Add to that the cost of utilities, transportation, entertainment, etc. Finally, that does not account for anything else such as medical costs that could significantly increase later in life. Accordingly, Social Security income must be supplemented.

In the past, most employees received a Defined Benefit Plan, also known as a Pension. In those days, the combination of Social Security and Pension payments were often sufficient for retirement living. More recently, Defined Benefit Plans have been replaced with Defined Contribution Plans also known as 401(k) plans and similar. The problem is that where Defined Benefit Plans (Pensions) guaranteed a retirement income for life, Defined Contribution Plans promise nothing, including they don't even help the retiree with converting an accumulated sum of money into an income they cannot outlive. In effect, the shift in plans was a shift in message from "*Don't worry. We'll take care of you for life in retirement, and thank you for your years of service.*" to "*Good luck with that and don't let the door hit you on the way out.*"

In response to this philosophical shift, Nobel Prize winning economist Robert Merton published a paper (*The Crisis in Retirement Planning*, Harvard Business Review, July-August 2014) that excoriated corporate America for it. Merton argued that retirees do not need an uncertain lump sum of money but rather a reliable *paycheck* each and every month from the point of retirement onward for as long as they live. But as life expectancies increase, not only does a permanent income need become ever greater, so does the probability of a single catastrophic event that could destroy a person's retirement and threaten that they might outlive their money.

Many investment firms tout a solution of living off growth on principal. This is known as the "4 Percent Rule." Developed in 1994 by William Bengen, it assumed a portfolio of 50% stocks and 50% bonds that generated income based on 4% of principal, adjusted annually at an inflationary rate of 3% per year, was sustainable.

However, particularly in light of the Dot Com correction of 2000—2002 and the Great Recession crash of 2008, this strategy has been repeatedly and increasingly called into question by a multitude of economists, including Nobel Laureate William Sharpe. The collective result of these re-examination studies is that following the 4% Rule results in a greater than 50% chance of total failure and that sustainability is more appropriate at a withdrawal rate of 2.8%. Apart from the high danger of outliving your money, most people could not actually live on just 4% (much less 2.8%) withdrawal of their 401(k). Unfortunately, most investment advisers have little or no knowledge of the economics behind boiler-plate recommendations (like "*live off 4% of your principal*") and lull their clients into a false sense of security until a major market correction occurs and their entire retirement plan is destroyed.

Insuring one's retirement income is a simple way to *guarantee* it will always be there no matter how long it is needed. In fact, it's the *only* way this can be done and the *only* thing which can guarantee income for life is an annuity. These insurance products were covered in Chapter 8 (Annuity Myth Busting) but here the emphasis will be on their use specifically to insure lifetime income.

As a review, there are several different kinds of annuities, roughly grouped into two broad classes: Fixed and Variable. Both types offer income-generating capabilities, each benefitting circumstances for which they are ideally suited. But different annuity products offer a variety of different income generating strategies. Our job here is not to make a recommendation but to inform. To get a recommendation, seek an independent insurance professional with wide and unrestricted access to the universe of annuity products.

Traditional Annuitization—This is where an accumulated sum of money is converted into a guaranteed series of payments. Those payments may be monthly, quarterly, semiannually or annually and structured for a stated term. That may be for the life of one or two people (generally spouses), for a stated number of years (e.g., 5, 10, 15, 20, etc.) or a combination of both. One of the common criticisms of annuities is that "*If you die, the insurance company keeps all your money.*" This is an unfortunate mischaracterization of the "Life Only" annuitization choice. When an annuity is annuitized, the size of the payments varies based on the term. Thus, a single life income schedule pays more per month than joint life which pays more than joint life with 20 years minimum guaranteed. Thus, if a life only (called "life certain") annuitization schedule is elected, you take the risk of under-living your life expectancy. Conversely the insurance company takes the risk that you outlive your life expectancy (because they will end up paying you a lot more than what the annuity is worth). More than any particular payment schedule, the key is these payment schedules are your personal choices.

Income Riders—In recent years, a number of annuities, most often Fixed Index Annuities, have begun offering an annuitization-like feature that guarantees lifetime income but does not take away the cash value if you die prematurely. In some cases, the underlying account value can continue to grow even while the income is being distributed. Generally, the amount of monthly income is less than traditional life only annuitization, but it resolves the "*what if I die early*" dilemma. Further, some carriers offer as a secondary benefit to amplify the lifetime income stream for Long Term Care and other specified medical needs. As such, these income riders can provide a double level of protection in that not only is baseline income guaranteed, but can significantly increase if there is a major medical need. Finally, some carriers offer inflation-adjusted income increases. Generally, this choice starts off at less income than with election of level income, but in a period of high inflation, this feature might be very beneficial.

Penalty-free Withdrawal—While annuities are time deposits, they do not "lock up" your money for years upon years. With rare exception, they offer penalty-free access to a stated portion, commonly 10% per year and permit that withdrawal to be established as an automatic monthly draw if you wish. This offers several benefits including continued growth despite the withdrawals. The income amount may also be increased or decreased or even terminated as needed and exercising this withdrawal does not interfere with your future choice to exercise an income rider or even trigger traditional annuitization.

Required Minimum Distributions—Like any type of financial account, an annuity may be established as an IRA. At times, there are distinct advantages in using an annuity to hold an IRA, particularly a Fixed Index Annuity which pairs growth potential with principal protection. All IRAs are eventually subject to a mandatory liquidation by Required Minimum Distributions (RMDs), typically starting at age 70½. Apart from anything else, the schedule of RMDs generates an income which: 1) cannot be outlived (it's mathematically impossible to fully deplete an IRA based on the standard RMD table), 2) can provide increasing payments throughout life as long as the average rate of growth can keep pace with the RMD schedule. Within the broader scale of income planning, a projected schedule of RMDs becomes an essential component.

MONEY SECRET: Good income planning starts with a consideration of income sources that are guaranteed and permanent. Those include Social Security, Pensions and annuities. Only after a baseline income, including a "cushion" for unexpected increases is established and can last for life, then is it reasonable to explore ways to increase wealth. All commercial airlines tell this before every flight: "*Put your own Oxygen Mask on first.*"

CHAPTER 17
FUTURE OF THE JOB MARKET

Our world is changing at an ever-increasing rate. Globalization and technological advances create new opportunities but also makes yesterday's "cutting-edge" tools obsolete. To keep up, some have proposed streamlining education, making college three-years to a degree, rather than a four-year process (or 5 plus years for many), while others advocate for increased specialization in higher education.

A generation or two ago, it was common for students to "follow in their parent's footsteps" to continue a family career or business. Increasingly today, students enter college without a firm idea or focus of what they want to do after graduation. But this lack of a career goal combined with a corporate culture than can force multiple career changes during a lifetime makes a broad-based education more essential. Not only does breadth and diversity keep students current, if and when they decide (or are forced) to switch careers, it teaches them to think for themselves.

But this technology explosion is a two-edged sword. While it creates new opportunity, it also distracts and disrupts interactive communication, interfering with the ability to collaborate and communicate. Social scientists tell us that only 8% of communication is verbal. A much larger percent is through body language, tone and eye contact; none of which can be done with a text message. Thus, while information and information technology is today's top developing economic engine, effective communication remains a critical skill that is being lost. Think about the difference between talking to a computer and talking with a human-being.

Primary education is structured. Because of strictly regulated core requirements that consume a student's time, college-bound high school students cannot easily expand the length of their school day to add another class, or take more electives. College then becomes where a student can finally branch out and take classes in widely different areas that broaden their base. Thus, college offers insights into areas other than the initially chosen path. It's the foundation of the liberal arts education. Increasingly a high-school diploma (or less) is not a complete path to a career other than menial or blue collar labor. Invariably, some advanced education is necessary for earning more than minimum wage.

Globalization and communication also makes language more important than ever. The U.S. lags way behind other countries in language diversity knowledge. In fact, the country with the world's largest English-speaking population is China. Foreign language proficiency is not just about knowing Spanish, for example, to communicate with the Hispanic workers and/or consumers in your home town. It's about international sales, trade, science and business. While it is possible to get by on just English, throughout the educated world there is an enormous advantage to being able to communicate with others in their own language.

In business, the major foreign growth markets are Europe and especially Asia. But any business looking to grow itself must look to all foreign markets. All the world's economies are aging except Africa where the number of young consumers is disproportionately increasing. Students coming out of college, especially with business and entrepreneurship in mind, will find the rapidly developing opportunity abroad increasingly attractive, even if they never relocate beyond the borders of their home town.

On the other hand, there is a segment of American society that seeks simplicity rather than the complexity and stress of this rapidly-changing world. For them, there are alternative strategies.

Community and two-year colleges increasingly offer many technical career paths (electricians, plumbers, HHVAC repair, Nursing, Computer technician, etc.). This training leads to jobs that cannot be replaced by robots, technology or machines. Manufacturing today often requires skills that include both mechanical and computer training.

In addition, there is also a rising cottage industry rebellion, spurred by a backlash against all the technology. Increasingly people seek alternatives to mass-produced, mass-marketed things. Their niche is a return to individualized, customized and hand-crafted products. Yet, even this return to yesteryear approach may require cutting edge 21st Century technology and training. It's one thing to produce a hand-crafted product. Finding a reliable customer base in a world when more and more consumers shop online, may spell trouble for the person who completely rebels against technology.

MONEY SECRET: Education is continual and cannot be "one and done." This is especially true for people who embrace the modern age of technology and globalization; continuing and expanding education is essential for those who want to keep up. Most workers will face significant job changes or career changes during their lifetime of work. Conversely, technical professions provide a "safe harbor" for those who do not want to run in that "rat race." Finally, the entrepreneurial spirit is still strong, perhaps becoming stronger because it will be a necessary trait for success in generations to come. Regardless of a chosen path, education and training will remain the cornerstone of a person's ability to grow and adapt. Whether traditional, technical, community, or even online schools, it's never too late to learn something new.

CHAPTER 18
BUILDING INCOME BRIDGES

During our working years, we live on monthly income from employment. For most of us, it's reliable and predictable for the future. It's why losing a job is so stressful: "*How will the bills get paid?*" "*How can I provide for my family?*" "*What will I do now?*" But when we retire, many of these same worries are revisited. The only difference is that one is planned and the other is forced upon us.

The biggest difference between our working and retirement years is when we're working, tomorrow's income is from what we do today. When we're retired, tomorrow's income from what we did yesterday.

In previous chapters we've emphasized the importance of generating a reliable, lifetime income, including to make wise elections of when to start Social Security and using income annuities to fill in any inadequacy not covered by Social Security or pensions. However, one of the reasons people don't heed the advice to delay Social Security income until 70, or follow other recommendations, is because they don't see the bigger picture. Their fear of outliving their money and having no income creates stress like that felt if they suddenly lost their job.

Even retirees with sizeable nest-eggs feel genuine stress at where will tomorrow's paycheck come from.

If this is you consider the following: metaphorically, you may feel as though retirement looks like you're approaching the edge of an income cliff. The ground you were on while working was high, solid and the "view" was great. But at retirement, suddenly you feel like you're looking across a vast income-chasm with a thousand foot drop with no end in sight. You know all the "conventional wisdom" but it doesn't seem to apply so you ignore it all and tap whatever income resources you can, thinking at least doing so will lessen the plunge you're certain is coming. But, what you don't see is that only a short distance ahead, there's another income plateau, just as high if not higher than where you are on now. All you need to do is get there and you're safe. All you need is an income bridge.

Financially, many people don't realize they have developed resources to adequately span that gap. The challenge is in knowing how to do it and that's where the three biggest retirement myths disrupt sound planning.

1. **Myth #1:** "*Start your Social Security income as soon as possible because it won't be there for you later if you wait.*" The truth is that Social Security income, once earned is not and cannot be taken away. It's your money and despite the common cynicism about "greedy, heartless government politicians" who break promises, there are some things they cannot pull back and this is one of them.

   For most people, the earliest you can start Social Security is 62. For widows, it's 60. But depending on the year of your birth, full retirement age (FRA) is from 66 to 67 and the maximum retirement age is 70. By starting Social Security early (before 70) you lose 8% per year. Thus, starting Social Security income at 62 instead of 70 will result in a 64% reduction you'll never get back. For widows, the penalty is even bigger and then there's the second penalty for earning income, even part-time before your full retirement age. (These were covered in Chapter 3).

   Ultimately, building the income bridge starts with delaying Social Security income until 70. The two exceptions are: if *your* health is poor (*not* the health of a past relative) and you don't expect to live to a normal life expectancy, or if after careful analysis, there is no other solution (meaning you can't buy groceries or pay your heating bill without it).

2. **Myth 2:** "*Don't take any of your retirement account money until absolutely necessary (Required Beginning Age) and then don't take more than your Required Minimum Distribution demands because the taxes are terrible.*" First of all, IRA accounts are always taxable, so you don't avoid taxes by delaying. All you do is kick the can down the road, potentially making the tax problem worse by growing the IRA and passing it to your heirs whose tax liability upon each year's distribution is "less friendly" than yours. The other issue is that the taxable income from Required Minimum Distributions can adversely impact how much of your Social Security income is also taxed. Hence taking retirement distributions while delaying your Social Security can have some tax advantages.

Spending down your IRA before the start of Required Minimum Distributions (at 70) serves to reduce your future income tax rate, especially if done before starting Social Security.

Also, because tax brackets are by "steps" meaning if you are in the 15% top marginal tax bracket, increasing taxable income up to but not beyond the next threshold of the 25% bracket (based on 2017 schedules) does not alter your tax load. For example, a married couple can have up to $75,900 of taxable income (in 2017, after deductions) and still be taxed at the 15% tax rate. Thus a couple reporting $65,000 (after deductions) can still take $10,900 out of an IRA without bumping into the next (25%) bracket. Moreover, if that couple takes $1 "too much" the only thing taxed at the 25% rate is that $1. The rest is still taxed at 15%.

However, the tax rate problem can increase after a spouse dies. The reason is that tax rates for a single person are lower than for a married couple. For example, where (in 2017) the 15% tax bracket for a couple ("married filing joint") is up to $75,900, for a person filing single, it is $37,950. Thus, a widow (or widower) who was at the 15% tax rate with an income of $65,000 when married is now taxed at the 25% rate for on $27,050. Thus, taking larger distributions from an IRA while married may allow you to remain at a lower tax bracket after you lose your spouse.

3. **Myth 3** comes in two, diametrically opposed versions:
   Version 1. "*Required Minimum Distributions are a fixed percent.*"
   Version 2. "*Required Minimum Distributions will liquidate an IRA account over the course of your lifetime.*"

   The schedule of Required Minimum Distributions is based on a table of divisors. These numbers are divided into the value of the IRA as of the end of the business day on December 31 of the *previous* calendar year. Your applicable divisor is determined by your age on December 31 of the *current* year. For example, if you are 70 on December 31 of this year and because you were born from January 1 through June 30 (you're still 70 in the same year you turned 70½), your divisor is 27.4 which translates to a required Minimum Distribution of about 3.65%. Each successive year, the divisor gets smaller which means the corresponding distribution percentage gets bigger. This schedule continues through age 115 when the divisor is 1.9 and remains there for all years thereafter. Essentially, at age 115 and beyond, you're taking barely more than half each year of whatever is left in the IRA. At that rate, while the IRA will shrink rapidly, it is mathematically impossible to liquidate 100% of it.

By reversing the "conventional wisdom" and spending the IRA instead of Social Security, two things happen. First, the tax-advantaged Social Security income gets to grow at 8% per year, guaranteed, plus inflation for as long as possible (until age 70). Nothing else does that. Second, by taking distributions, your IRA becomes smaller, and therefore has less tax impact at age 70 when both Retirement Account Distributions and Social Security must begin.

For example, Bob & Mary, both 65 have just retired. Together, they receive a pension of $1500 per month and are eligible (at 65) for Social Security benefits totaling $3500 month. They need $5000 per month to live. They also have 401(k) accounts totaling $300,000.

Succumbing to the "conventional wisdom" myths and seeing no other way out, Bob and Mary "bite the bullet" and start their Social Security income, justifying that "at least it's enough." Over the next 5 years, they are also pleased that the 401(k) continues to grow at 5% per year. Five years later, it's worth $383,052 and will generate a Required Minimum Distribution of $13,980 (the equivalent of $1,154 per month). Let's assume no inflation so their regular income and income need are still $5000 per month ($60,000 per year). Now their total income is $73,980.

Even better is that only $27,613 of their Social Security is reported as taxable. Their Adjusted Gross Income is $45,613. Bob and Mary are happy.

But if they did it right and withdrew $3500 from the IRA from 65 to 70 ($210,000 withdrawn over 5 years) when Required Minimum Distributions start, the remaining IRA account produces a much lower RMD of $5076/year ($423/month). At the same time their Social Security income has increased to $61,716/year ($5143/month) and their *total* income has increased to $84,792, a net increase of $10,812. In addition, their taxable income has dropped to $73,520. In other words, their total income increased by $10,812 while their taxable income decreased by $8093. With Bob and Mary at the 15% top marginal bracket, their net (after-tax) income actually increased by more than $12,000 per year—and this advantage will continue for the rest of their lives.

Further, if Bob dies early, Mary gets Bob's SS which is now a lot larger because he waited to age 70. Also, if Bob and Mary were in a "traditional" marriage where Bob, being the primary income earner has a much larger Social Security benefit than Mary, at Bob's passing Mary may elect to receive Bob's Social Security instead of her own. Finally, if Bob and Mary were different ages, and Bob was the older, at his passing, Mary gets to combine Bob's IRAs with her own and take Required Minimum Distributions at her age (which has a lower distribution demand).

This strategy also benefits them in that Social Security income has no exposure to market risk. Unlike a typical 401(k) investment account, if there is a major market correction (like 2008) relying on the 401(k) account to supplement income for life incurs significant risk of lost income capacity. Further, the longer you try to live off a risk account, the more likely you will experience a market correction from which your income strategy may not survive. You have put yourself at risk for outliving your money. For this reason, it is prudent to minimize or eliminate market risk from a significant portion of the IRA, 401(k), etc.

Finally, if Bob and Mary have any non-IRA type investments they can grow without needing to spend for routine income, their plan is even stronger. If an emergency arises, they can access that money at a better tax rate (long term capital gains are taxed at a lower rate than ordinary income). And, if they don't need it, when they pass, that money will transfer to their kids with a Step-up in Income Tax Basis and be available to the children with no income tax exposure. That's not the case with IRAs.

MONEY SECRET: Good income planning sometimes means going against the "conventional wisdom" especially when that "wisdom" is not so "wise."

1. Defer starting Social Security income as long as possible, preferably to age 70.
2. Use IRA (401k, etc.) or other income to bridge the divide between the time of retirement and Social Security election at the maximum benefit amount (70).
3. Increase your retirement account distributions based upon your AGI, but stay within your current tax rate.
4. Where possible, take steps to remove the IRA from market risk and secure the base (principal) so the RMDs, though reduced by spending, do not go away due to market corrections.

CHAPTER 19
YOUR NEEDS PLANNING

You know that you should have long-term "needs based planning" but you may not fully appreciate what that really is. The financial services universe consists of three industries: banking, securities and insurance. In the past, these were separate and held at arm's length.

Each industry served a specific purpose and didn't try to do what the others did. There were even laws in place to bar industries from mixing (e.g., the Glass-Stegall Act of 1933).

But today, everyone wants to be the "one-stop" shop and many of those old ethical rules have been thrown out (Glass-Stegall was repealed in 1999 which helped give rise to the mortgage crisis of 2007 and the Great Recession in 2008). Today, these industries—and their practitioners (sales reps) see the others as competitors (or worse) and in an effort to corral as much money to their side of the fence as possible, have shifted away from a true fiduciary duty to their clients. Simply, a fiduciary duty means the client's needs are placed above all else regardless of whether exercise of that duty results in a sale or not. In effect, this constitutes a shift from personal planning to product peddling.

The problem gets exacerbated in that the financial planning world has become increasingly complex and with that comes the need for increasingly specific, if not specialized, solutions. Unfortunately, the most sophisticated, if best products of one industry are simply not available to members of the other two. That doesn't make the industry, or even the products, bad. But when the tools are limited, so are the possibilities. By analogy, if all you have is a hammer and nails, you are limited to building things that can be accomplished only with a hammer and nails. It's the square peg in a round hole thing.

For example, let's assume you have all your money at a bank and you mention to your teller the money market account is earning nothing. The teller suggests you talk to the bank's financial advisor who then recommends an investment portfolio derived from investment choices with which the bank has marketing agreements. Unfortunately for you, those investment choices are not ideally suited to you but since the bank advisor is employed by the bank and restricted to sell only bank-approved products, you end up buying something that isn't right. In this example, the bank's financial advisor just made the sale more important than your need. To be fair, members of all three financial industries commit this error.

The real problem is not with the product or even the industry but with captivity. Captivity occurs an advisor is limited by his/her employer to offer or sell only products available by that employer or even that one (of the three) industry. Thus, while that employer may have 1,000 different product choices in their portfolio, it also means they do not have access to the 35,000 that are not available to them. Even if an advisor claims they are "independent" if their licensing is limited to one industry (e.g., securities or insurance), their "independence" is limited to that of one industry. They are not truly independent and by definition, cannot give genuine fiduciary advice.

Worse is when the great rivalry between investment advisors and insurance agents gets in the way. Representatives of each industry will up-play their own and down-play or even denigrate the other. Despite what they may say, it's not true that the "other guy's" products are terrible. Rather, it's that the person saying those bad things cannot sell them. They are biased.

Within the trifecta of financial industries: Banking, Securities and Insurance, sometimes people include real estate as a fourth industry. But as already discussed (Chapter 4), apart from your primary residence, real estate transactions for profit are either an investment (flipping for profit) which is securities or a business (rental) which is not a "financial industry."

Fundamentally, all three financial industries are legitimate and all three serve a valued purpose. But:

No one financial industry is right for everyone and no one financial industry is right for anyone's every dollar.

So how do you avoid the biases associated with captivity?

1. If they're affiliated with one of the "big name" firms that everyone knows, they're probably captive.
2. Ask. And specifically ask about the *other* industry's products. If the rep's answer is a broadly negative response (e.g., "*Annuities are terrible*" from an investment representative or "*Don't invest anything in the stock market*" from an insurance agent), that person probably has a bias.
3. Judge how the first session proceeds. If the advisor quickly jumps to product recommendations, especially before having done a thorough needs analysis, it's probably product peddling. By contrast, a genuine planner will start with a thorough and detailed examination of where you are now, where you want to go, what you have, and what your individual circumstances are. It involves good listening and a genuine effort to learn the particulars of your individual situation. This fact-finding doesn't have to be formal and certainly not an interrogation, but you definitely should be providing a lot of detailed information before the advisor starts "selling."

And the questioning should be a lot more than about how much you want to chase returns. It should include questions about family dynamics, income adequacy, both now and in the future, medical considerations including Long Term Care planning, inheritance planning and good general estate planning (note the operative word here is "planning").

4. Finally, the planner should be able to recommend specific solutions that can include components from all three industries without preconceived bias for or against one industry. The importance of this is not just that the recommendations are more specific and generally better. It's also that this indicates the advisor can offer flexibility, not just today, but for years into the future.

   Commonly, when people work with true professionals, they enter thinking they'll get one thing and exit doing something completely different that they never knew existed. And, at the end, their plan will not only meet their stated goals and be far better than what they initially expected.

MONEY SECRET: Work with advisors who are truly independent. They should have licensing in more than one industry, strong contacts with other professionals including legal and accounting, and who actively embrace the role of your fiduciary in making recommendations based exclusively on your best interests.

CHAPTER 20
UNDERSTANDING PROBATE

Most of us know that when someone dies, their assets will go through probate. Fewer fully understand what that is. What is commonly called "Probate" is actually two separate, though sequentially linked processes.

Probate is the presentation of a document to the Clerk of Superior Court which states a decedent's desires. The Clerk is then tasked with that duty to validate that document. In other words, Probate literally means "proving the will." Technically, in most cases, this is a relatively simple process. Most Wills are "self-proving" and are executed with at least two witnesses and a Notary. The Clerk simply has to determine if the paper presented is the "last" one signed by the decedent.

Estate Administration is process of determining claims, the order of payment, the filing of tax returns, and the eventual distribution of the estate. This is the process that can be time-consuming and expensive and what is commonly referred to as "probate" although technically it is not.

Combined processes of Probate and Estate Administration:

After a Will is delivered to the Clerk of Court, the Clerk first determines if that document is a valid Last Will and Testament. This is "the Probate." Next, the Clerk must determine how assets are to be distributed. While the Clerk's duty is to distribute the assets according to the wishes of the decedent, it's often not quite that simple. Essentially the court has a fiduciary duty with regard to creditors including the IRS and State Department of Revenue before the assets can actually be distributed. When a decedents wishes, as stated in the Will, are at odds with what is real, or lawful, that's where the probate horror stories arise. The tasks of Estate Administration include...

1. First determine if the assets listed as owned by the decedent were *really* owned by that person. Just because someone claims to own something, doesn't make it so.

   Property ownership can be thought of as belonging to one of two categories: those with formal title and those without. For example, a house, a car or a boat have a formal title that is registered and archived by the county and/or state. However, furnishings in the house as well as other personal property have no formal title. They are simply owned by virtue of possession, often within the confines of a titled asset.

   With rare exception, there is no need to "prove" ownership of untitled assets and as such, the probate court has little to say about transfer of those assets.

   But when titled assets are involved, it ultimately falls on the court to complete the transfer of title from the decedent to a new owner. Transferring title requires the signature of the owner, who is now dead. Therefore, the court must assume that responsibility and do so without bias. That's where the process can get bogged down.

   First, the court must determine if, in fact, the decedent was not only a true owner, but also the *only* owner. Often times, assets are co-owned and depending on the exact nature of that joint ownership arrangement, there may be conflicts with the Will provisions.

   For example, John and Mary purchase a vacation house as Joint Tenants with Rights of Survivorship. This means that whoever outlives the other has clear and exclusive title to the property. However, John and Mary divorce and Mary "gives" John the house but John forgets to change the title. John then remarries and writes a new Will bequeathing the vacation house to his new wife, Susan. When John dies, Susan believes the vacation house will be hers but it's not. Despite what the Will says, the vacation house belongs to Mary because at John's death, title transferred to her as sole owner.

2. Next, the court must determine if the beneficiaries listed in the Will and those persons appearing before the court claiming to be beneficiaries, actually are the same people.
3. Finally, the court must determine if there were any rightful beneficiaries who are minors, or incompetent, or were unnamed, particularly when there is no Will. Although similar to the previous test, it differs in that previously, the court did not actively solicit claimants, but here it does. This is why Estate Administration is a public process. It gives anyone with a claim to step forward and be heard.

These latter two proofs are the source of some of the most bitter if not infamous probate fights there are.

For example, the popstar Prince died without a Will. Soon after, his one and only sister filed for inheritance of her brother's estate. This would have been the logical sequence. But soon after five other half-brothers and half-sisters also filed claims to the estate. Then, so did a half-niece, then a half-grand-niece and the parade continued. Even if Prince had a Will, the ensuing fiasco would have occurred because the other parties were afforded the right to file a claim and be heard. Prince died on April 21, 2016, and the court assigned a deadline of September 12, 2016 for anyone who wished to file a claim against the estate. As of November 25, 2017, the case had still not been finalized although it was speculated that half of Prince's $300 Million estate will be lost to the process.

Ultimately, it's the job of the court to make sure the wishes of the decedent are followed and the law is carried out. But when there are conflicts or contradictions, the court must make a decision based on law and sometimes that means "setting the Will aside". The two main reasons a

Will is set aside are that the decedent did not have the requisite capacity to execute a Will or that the decedent was "unduly influenced" by a person or persons who unfairly benefited by that "influence." Unfortunately, the process of proving the Will can be costly when there is a Will contest.

Estate Administration always includes the costs of court that can be several thousand dollars (for example, up to $6,000 in North Carolina; other states can cost more). There are also expenses associated with performing title searches, property appraisals, preparing tax returns including both an income tax return and estate tax return (IRS Form 706). And, if there are any challenges to the Will, not only must the estate have legal representation paid by the estate, the estate must also pay for legal counsel for all claimants. In other words, the estate pays for everything *before* the rightful beneficiaries get *anything*. There are many such cases where after all the expenses got paid, there was no estate left to go to the heirs named in the Will.

In 1996, Boston Red Sox legend Ted Williams signed a Will saying he wished to be cremated and have his ashes spread at sea. But after his death, the executor of his estate and two of his three children produced a hand-written piece of paper in which he claimed he wanted to be cryogenically frozen. However, his eldest daughter disagreed and fought against this. After a lengthy and expensive probate battle, the Will was set-aside and Ted Williams (technically just his brain) was cryogenically frozen. The entire estate was consumed by legal fees.

What makes a Will Valid?

1. Sometimes people believe that having no Will means they have no probate. In a way, that's technically true, but it does not mean what they think. Remember, there are two processes: Probate and Estate Administration. Whether there is a Will or no Will, the estate requires administration. However, when there is no valid Will, all States have a default version known as "Intestate administration." Unfortunately, the rules of Intestacy commonly do not conform with what a decedent would have wanted or the heirs expect, or even think "fair." Normally

the state's plan has a defined shared arrangement and it's one plan fits all.

2. Anyone who is competent can execute a Will. All that's needed are two signatures and a notary block. This is called a "Self-proving Will." Many people understand about the signatures but neglect to get those signatures notarized. Without the notary block, the Will is considered invalid and can be corrected *only* if all the original witnesses are located and appear before the Clerk to confirm their signatures.
3. With limited exception, only an original Will is valid. If the original is lost, even though a copy is available, it doesn't matter. The court may consider the copy invalid because presumably the original was destroyed by the decedent in an effort to revoke it. However, some states, under some circumstances, may permit a copy to be probated, but the process can be very difficult.
4. Sometimes people make minor changes by crossing out and correcting an item. However, even one such minor adjustment can invalidate the Will. The only legal way to change a Will is with a formal amendment known as a "Codicil" which is signed with the same formality as the original Will.
5. **Quality of drafting the Will.** As we've said so often before, two documents both called the same thing (e.g., "Will") can be vastly different in terms of their effect. Poorly drafted, incomplete or innocently simple Wills are notoriously ineffective, resulting in partial or complete intestacy. Moreover, because probate is "Statutory" meaning "laws of the States", a Will drafted in one state may not conform to the laws of another. The result could be intestacy. In addition, properties owned in multiple states will each be probated in the state of its location, not in the state where the decedent lived. Each process is separate and each process can be costly.

When a Will is drafted by and signed in a Lawyer's office, it has far more credibility than when drafted as do-it-yourself with a "Will kit" or by "online legal services." This is because the lawyer's job includes assessing the ability of the person to draft the document; that they're not mentally "losing it" or are not being unduly influenced, or any of the other common complaints that are raised by disgruntled beneficiaries as to why the Will should be set aside (and they are to be included).

Avoiding Probate.

While there are times when probate and estate administration are simple and "painless" processes, many estates, especially larger ones or those with "complex issues" are benefitted by avoiding Probate altogether. There are a number of ways to bypass this process.

Transfer by contract—Any asset held within a contract and administered by a neutral ("disinterested") third party, as long as the contract names beneficiaries will bypass probate. Examples include: life insurance, annuities, qualified accounts (IRAs, 401(k)s, etc.) and assets with certain joint rights designations (e.g., joint tenants with rights of survivorship, etc.) and Pay on Death (POD) and Transfer on Death (TOD) designations.

Transfer by Trust—Any asset that is *owned* by a properly funded Trust will bypass Probate. The critical key here is that the asset is actually owned by the trust, and not by the person who executed the Trust.

The value of avoiding probate is that bypass assets are transferred privately and cannot easily be challenged, if at all. For example, as already noted, when there is a Probate challenge, the estate must pay the legal fees of everyone including the challenger, regardless of the outcome. However, when a Trust is challenged, the challenger must pay his/her own legal fees. Also, trusts can be constructed with provisions that say *"If you challenge this, you get nothing."*

Trusts also offer more control of the distribution of assets than a Will. A Trust can establish and enforce a number of very specific distribution scenarios that are "if then." Similar provisional conditions cannot be created and enforced by a Will. The complex Will-based inheritance scenarios commonly seen on TV or in the movies are not actually accomplished by Wills but by Trusts.

Another advantage of Trust-based planning is that it can be completed while you are healthy and not under duress. Working with an attorney gives you a chance to learn what will be done, how much it costs, and even an opportunity to negotiate the price and details of the trust. The worst time to negotiate the price of estate transfer is after the Will-maker dies. Not only is it a time of stress, there is no chance of making changes or correcting mistakes; the game is over.

There are costs associated with probate and estate administration. For example, probate attorneys commonly get 5% of the estate in probate. For an estate worth $1,000,000, that's $50,000!

MONEY SECRET: Probate and Estate Administration avoidance can be valuable planning strategies but it's not quite as simple as some people believe.

1. Know what your options are and take advantage of the best strategy.
2. Shop around. It's OK to talk to more than one law firm to see what they'd do and how much they'll charge. But don't be taken in by a lower price. You generally get what you pay for. A more experienced attorney may give much better advice, options you don't know about, and accomplish your goals, even if it costs a little more.
3. Don't procrastinate. Far too often, people continually "kick the can down the road" because planning for the inevitable is an uncomfortable reminder that there IS an inevitable.
4. Once the plan is established and the documents drafted, put them in a safe place that your heirs know about and can access.
5. Hold periodic reviews. Nothing remains constant forever and good planning requires being able to reassess and adjust.

CHAPTER 21
BUYING VEHICLES

After a house, for most people, buying a vehicle represents the largest purchase you will make. It's also the largest financial transaction you will do repeatedly throughout life and depending on your preferences, perhaps as often as every few years. From a pure cost (capital loss) standpoint, new car buying is the most expensive option because with rare exception, the car's value car drops constantly, starting from the moment you drive it off the dealer's lot.

Car buying is made worse in that car dealers can be notoriously untrustworthy, especially the smaller independent ones. In large part, this is because there are few, if any, regulatory or ethical guidelines over what the profit margins are, how well represented the car's actual condition is and whether a particular car is really what it's represented to be. These potential problems are especially true when purchasing used ("pre-owned") cars.

New cars:

Some people absolutely want to drive a new car. They enjoy the fact that nobody else has owned the car before them, they love that "new car smell" and they believe buying a new car will eliminate the possibility they just paid for a lemon. Unfortunately, even buying a new car does not mean the car will be trouble-free although new cars come with strong warrantees and at least if there is a problem in the first few years of ownership, the repairs will not directly add to your cost. However, even under the best of circumstances, there is the inconvenience of having to take your car to the dealer and either wait while it's repaired or arrange for a loaner, which is then swapped out when you return to the dealer later to get your own car back.

A new car is invariably more expensive than used and starts to depreciate from the moment you drive it off the lot. Car dealers often advertise they sell cars for less than anyone else. Those ads, especially on TV by fast-talking, loud sales people, urge you to come on down today and take advantage of the savings they and they alone will give you. Compared with the rest of the world, Americans are *not* skilled at or comfortable with haggling the price of things. But financially, not employing this skill can cost you thousands of dollars.

The good news is that knowing even a few tricks, can save you a lot of money on the purchase of a new car.

1. **Buy your car on the last day of the month**. On the last day of the month, the dealership is trying to make their monthly quota and if they're a bit short, you have a better opportunity to negotiate. But you've just got to be willing to say "*Let me think about it and maybe I'll come back next week.*" And when the sales person says "*Let me check with my manager.*" that's code for the current asking price is too high and can be negotiated.
2. **Buy in the fall after the next year's models have come out.** In the eyes of the dealership, you're buying a year-old car that they have to clear off the lot to make room for the new models.
3. **Buy out-of-season vehicles.** For example, buy a convertible in the winter when the demand for that design is lower.
4. **Buy an over-stocked or mass-marketed vehicle** with a customer cash incentive, typically higher in summer or winter. Sometimes, dealers order a supply of cars that don't sell as well as they predicted. Those vehicles must be "unloaded" to make room for more popular ones.

5. **Be wary of "zero down, zero interest" financing deals.** The dealer is not offering you a zero interest loan to buy the car. What they've done is increase the asking price to include the interest in the sale. In America, by law, every new vehicle sold must display the MSRP (Manufacturer's Suggested Retail Price) which is set by the manufacturers. However, it is exactly what it says "*suggested*" and that does not mean it is the lowest the dealer can go and still make a profit. Being willing to buy the car outright may result in a lower purchase price. And, if you don't have that much cash available, check with your bank. Sometimes, borrowing the money from them to purchase the car can result in a better net cost.
6. **Do your research.** Before you buy, look up the Fair Purchase Price of the vehicle you want. The Fair Purchase Price is a weekly update on what consumers are actually paying for a particular make and model including the price range (low to high) and market conditions that affect those sales.

Leasing:

For some people, leasing is a better deal than buying. The key is in the number of miles you drive each month. If you do not put a lot of miles on a car each year (e.g., up to to 7000 miles per year) leasing can save you a lot of money as well as save you the hassle of haggling the price. Technically, when you lease a car, you "rent" it. The typical lease agreement is for three years and the leasing price is set, in part, by the number of miles you intend to drive. The fewer miles you intend to drive, the less the cost. But don't understate your intended mileage. If you return the leased vehicle with a lot more miles than you agreed to, you pay a penalty in addition to the turn-in fees. When you turn the vehicle in, you get to renew your lease agreement with a new car. Thus, leasing is an easy way to always drive a car that is three or less years old, and it's a lot less expensive overall than purchasing a new car, even including the trade-in value when you buy the next one. Be aware that the turn-in fees can be higher than expected, including having to replace the tires. You also have the option of purchasing the vehicle at a pre-determined price that can be favorable.

However, if you drive a lot of miles (e.g., 7000 or more per year) or love to buy new and "drive it into the ground", leasing is a poor option.

Used cars:

If you are willing to drive a car that was previously owned by someone else, buying used ("pre-owned") can result in substantial savings. Of course, the challenge with buying used, apart from the emotional issue of not being "the first owner" is condition and reliability. Used cars commonly are sold because someone is trying to unload a car with problems, especially before they become overtly obvious.

However, there are a number of ways to guard against buying a "lemon" or even overpaying for a used car.

1. **Do your research**.
    a. Get a free CARFAX report (https://www.carfax.com/). All you need is the VIN (Vehicle Identification Number) and the CARFAX report will tell you if the vehicle was involved in an accident or was damaged by a storm or flood, etc. But do your own inspection because this report can be flawed.
    b. Check with the National Highway Traffic Safety Administration (NHTSA) website (www.SaferCar.gov) to see if there are any outstanding recalls.
    c. Test drive the car. Look for signs of damage and listen for "funny sounds." If you have a favorite auto mechanic, take the car there for an independent inspection and assessment.
    d. Look up the Kelley Blue Book retail value of the car. The actual value will be determined by make, mile, miles drives and individual condition. Knowing what the fair market range is for a particular make and model before you show up on the lot, will go a long way toward knowing if you're getting a fair offer or not.
2. **Warrantees.** Buying a used car with a warrantee is usually better than not. However, be careful. Some warrantees are better than others. Best

is a continuing manufacturer's warrantee. Next is a dealer's warrantee. Last are extended warrantees that a consumer has purchased. Some cars, especially those with a salvage title, cannot be warrantied, even by purchasing an add-on ("extended") warrantee. That's not to say it's necessarily a bad idea to purchase these cars. However, it does mean you must be careful, know what you're doing and be willing to accept the risk of having to fix something major that you weren't aware of.

3. **Buy a rental**. One of the best kept secrets about buying used cars is to buy the car from a rental company, especially the big-name companies. Every time you rent a car, after you turn it in, the car is washed and serviced. The level of maintenance on a rental is generally much higher than on a "regular" car that someone else owned and drove, day in and day out. And rental cars are kept one year and then sold. Therefore, buying a rental car generally means you are buying a well serviced car that is one year old and still under the manufacturer's warrantee. While you may pay a little more for all the service and cannot haggle their price, you may do better overall. This is because rental companies buy cars in volume so they start with a better purchase (to them) price then got revenue from the rents.

    Another advantage of buying from a rental company is their inventory is generally much larger than that of a typical dealer. And, if the car you want is not available on the lot where you are, the company can search their national database and find one elsewhere that can then be transported to your location.

    The one disadvantage of buying a rental is that most rental cars are not purchased with a lot of bells and whistles. So, if you are looking for a lot of options, you may have a difficult time getting what you want. However, if you're looking for the "mainstream" package and want reliability, this is an excellent option that is often not considered.

4. **Buying from a car warehouse**. Many large volume retail operations advertise they sell cars for a better price. Essentially what they're doing is buying in bulk and passing some of the savings onto you. However, a good negotiator (haggler) may do better with a traditional

dealer (seller of a particular car manufacturer) than a used car warehouse which won't haggle. Also, if you prefer a specific make and model car, you may find a better selection at the dealers (for that car manufacturer). But, regardless of how big a name the retailer enjoys, check the car out; test drive it, get a vehicle history report, check with the NHTSA for recalls, etc. There are areas of the country where cars may have been exposed to severe damage. For example, buying a used car that came from state shortly after a devastating hurricane or flood occurred there, may mean you're buying someone's storm or flood wrecked car. Such things will be revealed by doing a little investigative homework and the tell-all is the reports connected to the car through its VIN (Vehicle Identification Number).

Tax Deduction Opportunities:

Anytime you drive a car for business purposes, you may deduct the miles. For example, in 2017, the mileage deduction was 52½ cents per mile. So, if you drive your car 10,000 miles for business, the deduction is $5250. As noted in Chapter 4, business deduction miles cannot include commuting miles but other than that, the business miles can be for virtually any business, even a weekend business endeavor.

If the car is leased, taking itemized deductions rather than mileage may be more advantageous. In this case, you would need to keep records of your gas and maintenance receipts and you can also deduct the interest on the lease payments.

Business vehicles can also be depreciated but for most cars, up to maximum of $11,060 each year. However, if you purchase a passenger vehicle that weighs more than 6000 pounds or a truck that weighs more than 14,000 pounds, you can take a higher deduction. According to IRS Section 179, heavy vehicle deductions were 50% of the purchase price in the first year if taken in 2015-2017, then 40% in 2018 and 30% in 2019. Check with a CPA for the current status before assuming what your actual deduction may be, but knowing about the opportunity is half the battle won.

MONEY SECRET: Buying a vehicle starts with knowing your options and making good decisions on the approach and method that best suits your needs. Sadly, the last place to get good advice on buying cars is from the dealers. They have an agenda (to sell you a car) and they may not know all the best choices, even if the sales agent is willing to do that. Do your research and try to take the emotions out of buying a particular car.

CHAPTER 22
LAWYERS VS. FINANCIAL ADVISORS

Too many times, these two professionals operate at odds with each other. Sometimes financial planners make recommendations that contradict the plans lawyers put together and vice versa. There are many reasons why this occurs and it does not mean either the financial planner or the lawyer is acting in bad faith. It means they were not working together.

Both professions should complement each other but when that doesn't occur, it's often because each sees their role as competitive with the other. Lack of communication is then exacerbated by limitations each has on the knowledge and capabilities of the other.

For example, there was a case of a wife who needed long term care and the attorney was able to get her qualified for state government assistance. The husband had an account of more than $300,000 at the bank and at the suggestion of his banker, made a designation change to "avoid probate." Unfortunately, this one change was contradictory to the long-term care planning put together by the attorney and the banker's "help" disrupted that plan. It ended up costing the family over $100,000 in additional nursing home expenses.

On the other side, an attorney seeking to reduce a client's risk exposure steered that client toward an investment choice that the attorney knew about. In doing so, he also steered that client away from a financial strategy that was far better. Because the attorney/client relationship had been established before the client/financial advisor, the client was leery of and refused to take the financial planner's advice because it contradicted what the attorney said. When the markets went through a substantial correction, the client lost a third of his portfolio.

Many times a conscientious financial planner will tell a client "*You need a trust*" and the client goes shopping for the least expensive lawyer that can be found. The client then reports to the financial planner "*I got a trust*." and the financial planner responds "*That's good. You're in good shape now.*" Sadly, that's not necessarily true and in fact, that process may have made the client's situation worse. How? A Trust *must* be fully funded (meaning transfer title of all assets into the trust) to be effective and, as we've said so often, the details are everything. But in this case, what the client got was a boiler plate trust document (that lacked the necessary details) and an accompanying letter instructing the client to now go get the trust funded, which never got done. When the client died, not only did the estate get probated with all the expense of estate administration, it then went through trust administration. Each process has an associated expense, and this client's estate went through two instead of one. In such a case, one might argue that the financial planner was guilty of giving bad legal advice but that's not true. The financial advisor referred the client to an attorney which is all a financial planner can legally do. The client simply picked the "wrong" attorney. And because the financial planner took the client's word at face value, neither the client nor the financial planner knew the trust plan was not completed. And, the attorney's response was that he told the client, in a formal letter, what to do. If the client failed to do what was instructed, that's not his (the attorney's) fault.

In all these examples, the real fault is the assumption that a product (a trust and an investment recommendation) was the answer. But products, by themselves, are never the answer. What planning is really about is the dissemination of advice that is specific and tailored to the client and derived from a measure of expertise in that particular field. That advice, dispensed by the appropriate professional, not only far exceeds that of the client's knowledge and capabilities, but also of the other professional.

One of the reasons that professionals fail to make cross-recommendations is because each harbors a fundamental concern if they send you to the other, they'll never see you again (thereby losing a client or a sale). This business fear gives rise to a protective tendency that in effect says "*My client. Hands off.*" If asked, each professional will profess that they're following their fiduciary responsibility, justifying it to themselves, if not you, that they're protecting you from "predatory tendencies" of the other.

MONEY SECRET: There are many competent and ethical attorneys and financial advisors in the marketplace. Each serves the needs of their client with excellent advice in their respective fields. However, unless you find *both* who actively cooperate in the plan, you are not benefitted. Thus, it's not enough to just have a "good lawyer" and a "good financial planner." You must have both where they cooperate and collaborate with each other on your behalf, each lending his/her expertise to the equation.

CHAPTER 23
INHERITING MONEY

According to a 2013 study by Jay Zagorsky, an economist at Ohio State University, one in three people who received an inheritance had negative savings within two years of the event and the vast majority of people blew through it quickly.

For most people, that inheritance represents the one time in their lives that they will receive a windfall. In addition, most beneficiaries have little or no understanding about the tax consequences (good or bad) associated with inheriting money. That lack of knowledge can lead to poor financial decisions.

Step-up in income tax basis—When any asset of appreciated value is inherited, if that asset is not associated with a tax-deferred arrangement (IRA, 401(k), 403(b), TSP, annuity, etc.), that asset transfers to the heirs at its fair market value as of the date of death (or an alternate valuation date up to six months after). That means that the asset has a new income tax basis that is a substantial benefit to the heir. Consider how this works: Suppose you purchased an asset for $1000 and through time, it has grown in value by $100,000. The $1000 is called your "Basis" and the $100,000 is the gain or "Capital Appreciation." If you sell the asset, you must pay income tax on the Capital Appreciation portion but not the Basis. But when you die the asset passes to your heirs. If they then sell it, the inherited basis is $101,000 and no income tax is due. It's called a "step-up in basis." Note that literally, if the asset is sold one minute before you die, there is a tax liability and if one minute after, there is not.

Inheritance Taxes—Despite a popular "battle cry" from some politicians about a "death tax," there is no tax on dying (good luck collecting from the decedent). More correctly this refers to an Inheritance (or Estate) Tax which is a tax on wealth *transfer* from one person to another. However, in all cases, there are certain amounts of money that are exempted from inheritance tax that fall into two broad categories:

1. **Inheritance by a Spouse.** When someone inherits assets from a spouse, there is generally no estate tax issue because the surviving spouse enjoys an unlimited marital exemption. This may not be true if there are "strings" attached to the inheritance, such as with certain types of trusts. For example, some irrevocable trusts are specifically designed to retain this unlimited exemption. Some "strings" are okay and others are not as it relates to the exemption. If the spousal inheritance is exempt, then the inheritance is included in the surviving spouse's estate. If it is not exempt, the inheritance is included in the decedent's (first spouse) estate for tax purposes. In other words, if the unlimited marital exemption does not apply, then the inheritance tax, if any, goes by the same rules as inheritance by non-spouse beneficiaries.
2. **Inheritance by Other than a Spouse.** When anybody other than a spouse inherits assets, an estate tax liability is calculated on the entire amount. But the family gets an exclusion based on the Fair Market Value of all the property in the estate (less the unlimited marital exemption described above) for Federal Estate Tax purposes. This is called the Applicable Exclusion Amount. For example, in 2017, that exclusion was $5,490,000 (which is enjoyed by each spouse). Anything over that amount is taxed at the Federal Estate Tax rate of 40% (plus state where state inheritance taxes apply). So, with an estate worth $5,490,000 or less, no estate tax is due because the first $5,490,000 (or $2,196,000; 40% X $5,490,000) is exempted by virtue

of the exclusion. This is sometimes referred to as the Unified Credit so it's as though there is no estate tax due. Technically, there is; it's just "deducted away" by the unified credit amount.

But estates valued at more than the unified credit are subjected to estate tax, payable within 9 months of the date of death. For example, suppose your estate (in 2017) was worth $6,000,000 and you died that same year. The estate tax due would be $204,000 ($6,000,000—$5,490,000 = $510,000 X 40% = $204,000). For married couples, each spouse gets the exemption and the survivor can use the unused exemption of the deceased spouse if an estate tax return is filed upon the first death. Hence a married couple can leave almost $11 Million to their children (or others) with no Federal Estate Tax owed. However, some states do have a state inheritance tax that is tacked on top of the federal. The rates vary from state-to-state.

Gift taxes—As of 2017, anybody may make a gift to anybody of up to $14,000 (called the annual gift exclusion) per year and not need file a Gift Tax Return (IRS Form 709). However, when the sum of all gifts by one person to another person in one year exceeds $14,000, a Federal Gift Tax Return is required (it's filed at the same time as your regular 1040 income tax return) and the excess amount is taxed unless you file the return and use part of your lifetime exemption for the gifts. As noted above, everyone has a lifetime exemption of $5,490,000. Gifts, in excess of the annual gift exclusion reduce the size of your lifetime exemption.

While most people never file a Gift Tax Return, some people make large gifts for estate planning purposes. If so, any gift tax exemption you take is deducted from your exemption for the Estate Tax at your death. For example, suppose you have an estate worth $6,000,000, facing an estate tax of $204,000 (example from above). So you gift $1,000,000 to your son (after giving him $14,000). You file your Gift Tax Return taking the exemption of $1,000,000 then you die. Your estate's value has been reduced by $1,000,000 to $5,000,000, but so has your Applicable Exemption Amount—to $4,490,000 and your estate tax is still $204,000.

However, if the gifted property, after you gave it, grew from $1,000,000 to say $2,000,000, none of that appreciation is included in your estate for tax purposes.

Tax-qualified Accounts—Tax qualified retirement plans (IRAs, 401(k)s, etc.) are those plans funded with pre-tax dollars, permitted to grow tax-deferred and subject to a schedule of Required Minimum Distributions usually starting at age 70½. Because they were tax-deferred, they receive *no* Step-up in Basis at death and are 100% taxable as ordinary income to any beneficiary (you, your spouse, children, or others) other than a charity. Account owners can take distributions without penalties upon reaching 59½ and can withdraw any amount from their account. Spouses who inherit these accounts can roll over the account to take advantage of their own age for Required Minimum Distributions. No other individuals get that advantage. Recipients of inherited IRAs may not combine an inherited IRA with their own and may not defer Required Minimum Distributions until they reach the Required Beginning Age of 70½. Finally, unless specific steps have been taken to guarantee the inherited IRA will not be distributed rapidly (or in lump sum), heirs face the potential of receiving a very large IRA payout distribution which is fully taxable at ordinary income rates, including at the new tax brackets the beneficiaries just found themselves in. Unless Congress takes steps to undo it, there is a non-default allowance in the tax code that permits an inherited IRA to "Stretch" meaning it gets distributed according to the life expectancy of each individual beneficiary. However, making sure an IRA will successfully "stretch" requires taking specific steps that are generally not offered (or revealed) to IRA owners by their financial custodians.

Roth IRAs and Life Insurance—While completely different in all other ways, both provide an opportunity to accumulate and transfer moneys on an income tax-exempt basis. However, neither is exempt from inheritance tax exposure although (as previously discussed) life insurance can be made estate-tax exempt; Roth IRAs cannot.

Double Taxation—When large estates consist of mostly tax-qualified (retirement) money and are above the Lifetime Exemption amount, there is a real danger of double taxation. For example, suppose a wealthy widow with has an estate worth $6,490,000 which includes real estate and an IRA worth $1,000,000, the IRA being her only liquid money. Let's also assume (for our purposes here) that her son, her sole heir, earns more than $444,550 each year placing him in the top marginal tax bracket of 39.6%. At the point of inheritance, the IRA will be subject to two tax calculations. The first is an inheritance tax of 40% ($400,000) due within nine months of the date of death. To pay this tax, the son liquidates the IRS (his only choice because it must come out of the estate) and is now subject to an income tax of $396,000. Thus, the total tax liability is nearly 80% and that does not include state income tax if the son doesn't live in an income tax free state.

There is a provision known as "Income in Respect of a Decedent" (or IRD) under IRS Section 691(c) that permits the son to offset the inheritance tax against the income. However, this election is not automatic and must be elected and the IRS is not going to call them to say "*Hey, did you know...*"

Other considerations.

Issues with Inheritance protection arise from primarily two sources: Divorce and Scavengers (children and grandchildren).

- **Divorce**—Inherited property in most states is **Non-Marital Property**. If the marriage is not strong, keeping inherited property separate from joint or comingled property can protect it from being divided in the event of a divorce.
- **Scavengers**—It's really difficult for parents to say "no" to children and especially to grandchildren. So, when there is a large inheritance (or even a small one) and the kids say "*Mom I need a...*" it's because they know that mom just inherited a bunch of money from grandma.

Medical and Long-Term Care Needs also can be benefitted by inheritance. For most people, inheritance is a windfall that will not be repeated. It affords "breathing room" to complete critical planning that's been delayed due to other financial constraints. If there are any holes in complete planning, this is the right time to fill in those holes. For many people, there will not be another opportunity.

MONEY SECRET: When money is inherited, it's an asset and it should be handled as such. In most cases, it is also the last windfall a person will get in life and the last opportunity one may have to:

- Resolve serious financial issues.
- Pay off debt, especially high interest debt.
- Secure personal estate planning to take care of yourself, your spouse, and to give your legacy to your children and grandchildren in the best way possible.
- Protect your assets from harm including Long Term Care or major medical needs.

Do the important things before buying toys or chasing whimsical items on your "bucket list." Consult a tax professional to ensure there are no tax "surprises" in store and consult a financial planner to get some ideas about how to make the money work for your long-term benefit, and consult an attorney to take advantage of the kinds of planning that will secure your control now and for the future.

When that inheritance is used for those things, it may not be "sexy" or glamorous, but it will be worth far more to you in the long run than a fancy new car (or whatever stuff you might buy). Don't be like the masses who spend their entire inheritance in two years and have nothing to show for it.

EPILOGUE

In late December 2017, Congress passed a sweeping tax reform act. Among the many changes were adjustments to most of the marginal tax brackets, doubling of the standard deduction, elimination of personal exemptions and a doubling of the Unified Credit Limit (estate tax threshold). These changes (and more) may impact many of the tax considerations discussed herein. However, the law is scheduled to sunset (meaning go away) on January 1, 2026 at which time (assuming no further law changes occur), many of the new changes will largely revert to the way they were before the laws changed. In the Preface, we admonished that this book cannot be used for specific or individual tax advice. This is an example of why that is true.

ABOUT THE AUTHORS

William G. Alexander, Attorney

A native of Kannapolis, North Carolina, Bill graduated from Davison College and Wake Forest University School of Law (1976). As founding attorney of W.G. Alexander & Associates, PLLC in Raleigh, NC, Bill has over 41 years in practice, primarily in the area of asset protection, estate and elder care. Bill maintains an "A-v Preeminent" peer rating by Martindale-Hubble and a "10-Supurb Attorney" Avvo rating, the highest ratings offered. As a Veteran, he also became a VA accredited advisor.

Bill's practice was heavily influenced by his life circumstances. While a student at Davison, his brother was seriously injured in a traffic accident. Later, when his father died, he became his brother's Trustee and caregiver. In addition, he had to manage his mother's affairs through more than two years of long term care needs.

Currently, his practice focuses on business, including business strategies and families including asset protection, wealth transfers, Eldercare and crisis planning for long term care, as well as addressing the unique challenges faced by seniors, planning for the special needs community, estate planning with wills and trusts, including the handling of trust administration and probate. He also helps war period veterans and their families with long term care benefits.

Bill is a member of the Estate Planning and Elder Law Sections of the NC Bar Association and is currently active with the Mid-South Forum of Estate Planning Attorneys, WealthCounsel, ElderCouncil and the National Academy of Elder Law Attorneys (NAELA). He was named Elderlaw Attorney of the Year, 2011 and 2016 by the NC Chapter of NAELA and served as President of the State Chapter in 2013. A sought-after speaker, he provides advanced continuing education for Attorneys, CPAs, financial advisors, insurance agents, and health care professionals. He serves on the Board of the William Black Lodge, the Roanoke Island Historical Association Endowment Board and manages the Percy W. & Elizabeth G. Meekins Charitable Trust for the arts and education of Dare County, NC. He was been awarded the Legion of Merit, the Distinguished Service Medal, and the Order of the Long Leaf Pine, the highest award offered by the State of North Carolina. He is also a 32° Scottish Rite Mason.

Bill hosts the radio show "Asset Protection Today" and co-hosts the TV show "Money Secrets with Bill & Mike" produced by Uptone Pictures.

Michael Tove, Financial Planning Advisor

A native of Raleigh, North Carolina, Mike started life in the world of academia. After graduating from Guilford College, he earned his Master's Degree in Biology from Western Carolina University and his Ph.D. from Utah State University. Following a brief stint teaching, mostly at the public school level, he made a career shift into insurance and financial planning. He earned life and health insurance licenses and became securities licensed (currently as a Series 65 Investment Advisor Representative with CoreCap Investment Advisory Service). After becoming licensed, he trained with the National Institute of Certified Estate Planners and the College for Financial Planning and in 1998, founded AIN Services, a multi-faceted, fully independent agency focused on financial, insurance and retirement planning, asset preservation, long term care protection and general estate planning.

AIN Services is a member of the Better Business Bureau of Eastern North Carolina with an A+ Accreditation as well as a member of the National Ethics Association. Mike is a Certified Estate Planner and member of the National Association of Certified Estate Planners, a Registered Financial Consultant and member of the International Association of Registered Financial Consultants. In addition, he was inducted into the Independent Excellence Group, an elite think-tank organization composed of the top financial planning and wealth preservation professionals in the country and has qualified for membership in the Million Dollar Round Table since 2005, and is presently a Top of the Table member, the highest rank offered by that organization.

Mike is a prolific author, having actively publishing in both academic and popular literature dating back to the late 1970's. He has scores of publications to his credit, including has wrote two chapters in the book *"What You Don't Know about Retirement Income can Hurt You."* His numerous publications credits also include chapters in several books plus he is sole author of another in the areas of biology and wildlife, plus he has written and published fiction stories.

No stranger to the film and television industry (having worked as performer, writer and producer), he is the creator and co-host of TV Show "Money Secrets with Bill & Mike" produced by Uptone Pictures.

Made in United States
Troutdale, OR
11/03/2026

56852691R00106